The Fon of Bafut

The Fon of Bafut

PAT RITZENTHALER

photographs by Robert Ritzenthaler

THOMAS Y. CROWELL COMPANY

New York   Established 1834

Preface

In 1959 I lived for five months in the charming little village of Bafut in the Bamenda highlands of what was then the British Cameroons on the coast of West Africa. My husband, an anthropologist at the Milwaukee Public Museum, did what is known as a "village study" and gathered specimens for the museum. Although I am not an anthropologist, I was put to work transcribing notes, interviewing people, recording music, and taking pictures.

This is the story of an African boy who grew up to be a king. It is the story of his tribe, his traditions, his culture. There are multitudes of books concerning the political aspects of the "emerging" nations; I have described, rather, the traditional way of life of one small region on the huge continent of Africa. But it is my hope that an understanding of this remote area will prove helpful in furthering the reader's empathy with the rest of the continent.

In 1959 the Southern Cameroons was a United Nations trusteeship administered by England; it had been a ragtag bit of Nigeria from 1917 until independence in 1961, when the southern area voted to rejoin the former French Cameroun and became the Western Region of the Federal Republic of Cameroon.

When I knew it, the area was quite underdeveloped. The roads were poor, with only 125 miles of paved roads near the coast. During the rainy season, most of the inland area north of Kumba was cut off for weeks at a time. The rest of the year the clay and dirt road was traveled alternately, traffic going north one day and south the next, with Sunday reserved for road repair. There was no newspaper or other publication and no radio station. A transmitter from Lagos, nine hundred miles away in Nigeria, relayed news and music. North of Buea, the tiny capital, with a population of around three thousand, there was no electricity or telephone; communication between the grasslands and the outside world depended upon mail and telegraph. Even with the help of three mission groups in the fields of education and religion there was 96-percent illiteracy. Prior to 1948 there were no political parties. The men voted for the first time in 1955, the women in January 1959. All of this has since changed rapidly and is still changing.

In spite of these so-called primitive conditions, we discovered in Bafut a kingdom over three hundred years old, whose Fon (a paramount chief) held complete sway over some twenty thousand people. He already had been introduced to the world by Gerald Durrell in *The Bafut Beagles;* before that, his royal compound had been the showplace of the Cameroons for years. Intrigued though we were by Durrell's Fon, a swaggering, gin-imbibing, fun-loving chief, who liked to stay up half the night dancing with his numerous wives, we also found a man seriously concerned about the cultural changes rapidly taking place in his kingdom. We became acquainted with a people whose story was not well known, agriculturists who were being thrown unprepared into the fast-moving events of the new Africa.

With the exception of Achirimbi, Aboumbi, and other historical figures, the personal names of the narrative are not meant to depict the living or the dead; rather, the characterizations are based upon composite personalities. Some names have been deliberately misspelled and a few place names disguised to ward off the possibility of hurting any Bafut people today. The incidents portrayed are based on legend, historical fact, British Government reports, and our own observations. A partial account of Aboumbi's funeral, in somewhat different form, was published in the Milwaukee *Journal.*

Except for the picture of the Fon and Queen Elizabeth, which is separately credited, my husband is responsible for all the photographs, and they are reproduced through the courtesy of the Milwaukee Public Museum. The entire project was sponsored by the Friends of the Milwaukee Museum, Inc., and the Wenner-Gren Foundation for Anthropological Research. I also owe much to the valuable assistance and blessed friendship of the following:

Dr. and Mrs. Paul Gebauer, the late Dr. Melville J. Herskovits and Mrs. Herskovits, Dr. Phyllis Kaberry, Dr. E. M. Chilver, Mr. and Mrs. Stanley Marriott, Mr. and Mrs. Gilbert Schneider, and numerous other friends who were such a comfort while we were in the Cameroons.

Many Africans contributed to our education and physical welfare, particularly our steward, Joseph Kake, our interpreter, Martin Mfombe, our friends Rudolph and Lydia Ndifon, and the rest of the Bafut people. Without the perceptive assistance of the Fon of Bafut our work would have been in vain—and I would have had no story! To him and many of his wives I owe a special debt of gratitude.

But it is to my husband I owe the deepest appreciation for making it all possible: the trip to Africa, the understanding with which he taught me the comprehension necessary for living in another culture, and his love and patience while this book was being written.

Pat Ritzenthaler

Milwaukee

Contents

Illustrations

The Fon of Bafut

The Fon of Bafut

Parked at the foot of the resthouse steps, before the gates of the royal compound, the king's Land Rover awaited him. On its sides, lettered prominently, were the words *Fon of Bafut*. As usual, when the king planned a trip, most of his wives and children, as well as enchindas (young male servants), court messengers, and passersby, gathered around the vehicle. The four-wheel drive made this the surest means of travel in the grasslands. Even during the rainy season, when the mud often reached above the hub caps, the Land Rover could nearly always negotiate the difficult roads.

A young woman strolled out to the road. She was Lunda, one of the Fon's favorites among his younger wives. Her silk blouse was salmon-colored, and around her hips and reaching nearly to the ground she had wrapped a white skirt with black flowers on its border. Her hair had been tied into short braids, and these were bent into a halo, so that they trailed each other around her head. Over part of this coiffure she wore a bright turquoise scarf. She piled small rugs and pillows into the front seat, making it as comfortable as possible for her royal husband. Then, regally, she climbed up next to the driver, her chin pointing imperiously down the road to Bamenda.

Meanwhile, other wives were filling the rear of the Land Rover with all kinds of boxes, calabashes, gourds and bottles of palm wine, an alarm clock, and baskets of food. Into the back, too, went several wives, a couple of enchindas, and one of the princes, who was carrying the badge of the important man of affairs in West Africa, a briefcase. There they all sat, restlessly waiting for the king.

At last Achirimbi, the Fon of Bafut, appeared. His imposing

figure, more than six feet tall, was clad in a long white robe with gold stitching down the front and back. On his head was a pointed gold cap with a long golden tassel that fell into his eyes as he beamed and nodded at his audience. Dark European trousers, with brown shoes and yellow socks, completed his costume. He had worn eyeglasses for some years now, for the sight in one eye was nearly gone, and the doctor in Douala had been unable to restore it. This made it imperative that he cock his head sometimes in order to see out of the good eye. The resulting imbalance gave him an impious look that was always heightened by his mischievous grin—some said it was more of a leer.

Smiling broadly, Achirimbi made a short speech. He told his subjects he was going down to visit in Mamfe for a few days, that Chunga and Kweyifon would be in charge while he was gone, and that he hoped Agnes' baby would arrive before he got back. Everyone hooted at this. Agnes was awaiting her first baby, and every night for two weeks she had called her co-wives to come and deliver it. It hadn't arrived yet. The poor girl smiled tearfully.

When all goodbyes were said, the Fon regally waved a slender hand and climbed into his Land Rover. As it roared down the dusty road to Bamenda, scores of little royal children ran after it, screaming, pushing, and jostling, while the wives and enchindas waved their hands enthusiastically and called, "Walka good."

So it went every time Achirimbi went off on a motor trip. As a representative to the House of Chiefs in the capital at Buea, he made many trips between the grasslands and the coast. But he always returned to his mountain home with a great sigh of relief. He preferred, instead, the jaunts he took to other parts of the grasslands, where he conferred with tribal chiefs or government officials.

His longest journey had been a four-day auto trip to Lagos, Nigeria, in 1956, when he went to meet Queen Elizabeth. From the four paramount chiefs on the grasslands of what was then the British Cameroons, Achirimbi had been selected to present her with the tribute from her people.

Dressed in his finest robes and wearing his elephant-tail headdress, Achirimbi gingerly climbed the few steps that led to the veranda of Government House in Lagos. Through an interpreter, he murmured to the girlish figure standing before him that he was proud to bestow on her this gift: an elephant tusk exquisitely carved with the sacred symbols of the Cameroons—the spider, the leopard, the python, and the double-gong. Graciously, the queen smiled and accepted the gift; then, knowing how great a tribute it was, both for the work involved in its carving and for the rarity of the ivory itself, she suggested that it be returned to the people of the Cameroons. It would lie in their House of Assembly at Buea for all to see, a queen's tribute to her people.

The Fon smiled and thanked her. It was the sort of gesture he understood well, the noble gesture that made everyone happy.

In Lagos, Achirimbi saw more of the white man's trappings, of which he had become aware over a life span of nearly eighty years. Some he dismissed immediately as foolish and unworthy. Others, admittedly, had great merit: the white man's plumbing, for instance (although he kept losing his way in the hotel whenever he wanted to find the bathroom), and electricity, which he came away determined to introduce into his compound (although, to date, because of the lack of waterpower, it has been impossible to install). The museums at Lagos, Ife, and Benin he found stimulating, and he expressed the intention of starting a small museum of his own, possibly like the one built by King Njoya at Foumban in the French Cameroun.

With his usual discernment the Fon perceived the sad results of people rushing helter-skelter into great urban areas. He abhorred the noise, the poverty, and the filth of the Lagos slums. He feared the detribalization that is so often a by-product of city life. He loathed the degeneration of discipline and order, the lack of cohesion that occurs when men, either through economic necessity or extrinsic pressures, are torn from their tribal milieu.

Within his lifetime, Achirimbi ("He Who Lives Eternally"), monarch of twenty thousand members of the Bafut tribe in the Cameroons, had seen this happen. He had fought the white man—and had later submitted to him. He had been aware of the large cities, products of the white man's civilization, that had grown up along the coasts. He had seen the Cameroons pass from the Germans to the French and English. In a few more years, in 1961, he would witness the creation of the Federal Republic of

The Founding of Bafut

The Cameroons, ancestral home of the Bafut and many related tribes, got its English name from *camarãos*, the Portuguese word for the shrimp that abounded in the offshore waters. It was first sighted as early as 600 B.C., when Hanno the Carthaginian sailed on a voyage of discovery as far as the present Cameroons and described what is now presumed to have been volcanic Mount Cameroon. But not until the fifteenth century, when the adventurous Portuguese began to seek a route to the Spice Islands, was this majestic mountain, 13,353 feet high, noted again in the records. It was left to itself and to the native people, who slowly clustered around its lower slopes.

It is easy to find the Cameroons on a map of Africa. It lies in the elbow of the western coast, above the equator, where the coastline turns down from the huge bulge that is Northwest Africa to run almost due south. From the coast, which embraces the Gulf of Guinea, the land rises sharply to the summit of Mount Cameroon. Then it drops again to dense tropical forest, which gives way finally to a lovely plateau surmounted by more mountains.

Large and small feudal kingdoms abounded along the coast. Each of these native kingdoms had a strong central government, large armies, and many vassals. If one kingdom was not strong enough to protect itself, it was soon in servitude to its more powerful neighbor, paying taxes and tribute, supplying soldiers and slaves.

For Europeans, the Cameroons never possessed the exotic aura of romance that hung over the Nile, the Niger, and Timbuktu. The physical barriers alone were formidable: terrible mangrove swamps, rain forests, yellow fever, dysentery, and malaria—all of which gave the entire coast the reputation of being the "White Man's Grave." Coastal tribes added to the dangers by harassing the white men and preventing them from entering the interior, thus preserving their own status as middlemen in the ivory, oil, and slave trades.

The history of the Cameroons coast is the exciting, yet frightening, history of warriors, slavers, traders, and explorers. There were also such high-minded missionaries as Rev. Alfred Saker, who founded the little town of Victoria on the coast and fought steadfastly against slavery, illiteracy, and disease. There was, too, that turbulent English traveler of East African and Arabian fame, Richard F. Burton, who was the first to stand for an exciting moment on the summit of Mount Cameroon with Saker in 1862.

When Saker bought land from the Bakwiri and Isubu chiefs for his mission, he hoped that eventually England would become its protector. The traders, too, called for the strong arm of the British navy. Even one of the tribal chiefs, realizing that outside control was inevitable, wrote Queen Victoria for permission to visit England so that he could "become enlightened." Other chiefs, in 1877, wrote offering to surrender Douala, Bimbia, and Victoria if England would guarantee protection.

Although French traders were making forays all along the coast and the Germans, too, had begun to trade, the English were busy with territorial demands elsewhere in the world. Prime Minister Gladstone replied merely that the matter would be examined further.

It seemed the Prime Minister had turned a deaf ear to the pleas of Saker, Burton, the traders, and others, but there were some in the government who were convinced of the value of the area. T. V. Lister, in the Colonial Office, and Lord Granville, the foreign secretary, worked out a scheme to send Consul E. H. Hewett on a trip to report on climate, river channels, anchorage, drainage, and losses suffered by traders because of native quarrels. Although, as a result of Hewett's report, the government finally decided in favor of annexation, it delayed still longer in order to force the traders, who stood to gain financially from English protection, to bear the cost. But the traders stood firm, insisting it was a matter of national importance. By the time Hewett returned to Douala with treaties for the native kings, he was too late. The Germans had concluded their treaty seven days before.

While England was vacillating, Adolf Woermann, the leading German trader in the Cameroons, had gained an audience with Bismarck, the German chancellor, in 1884, and appealed for German annexation. Although Bismarck had made loud noises about not wanting a German empire, he recognized the soundness of Woermann's appeal and quietly dispatched Dr. Gustav Nachtigal to Douala to establish German rule.

The area that became the Southern Cameroons, or the western portion of the German Kamerun, was a rugged land. Roads were difficult to build and maintain—at one spot on the coast, Debundscha, the rainfall exceeded four hundred inches a year— but the Germans managed it with the help of native labor. It was an ideal land for bananas, coffee, oil palms, and cocoa. Huge plantations were developed, to become the base of the Cameroons economy. All of this necessitated a steady source of labor; that meant further exploration of the inland territory and further exploitation of the people there.

Today, when one drives from Victoria to the Bamenda escarpment, two hundred miles north, the stamina and fortitude of those traders, missionaries, and explorers seem almost unbelievable. But after the oppressive, dripping heat of the coastal rain forest, the men came to the lower slopes of the "Mountain of Greatness"—Mount Cameroon. Burton described his experiences on the mountain with such enthusiasm that one wonders why England didn't "protect" the area on the possibility of using its lower slopes for rest areas.

The Germans finally made Buea their principal headquarters, and until the consolidation with independent Cameroun in 1961, Buea remained the capital of the little Southern Cameroons. The Germans built a botanical garden at Victoria, where they conducted research on the wealth of tropical vegetation in their new colony.

In the relentless search for trade and laborers, the frontier was pushed farther from the sea. Having tramped through the coastal jungle and grimly climbed the forbidding mountains, the Germans finally emerged onto the plateau which is the grasslands.

Here they found a land entirely different from the coast. It was healthier, and it was thickly inhabited with tribes so linguistically diverse that often villages twenty miles apart could not converse with each other. Although there were great patches of forest, the grasslands were covered with thick, lush elephant grass, sometimes rising to a height of eight or ten feet. Game was still plentiful. Man, in his eagerness to burn the hills for farming and hunting, had not yet drained the area of animal life. There were forest buffalo (the bush cow so feared by the Bafut), leopards, antelope, tiny duiker (a species of small antelope), monkeys, cane rats, and elephants, which had not yet been forced to the coast. In 1855, Heinrich Barth, the famous German explorer, described one herd of ninety-five elephants at Lake Chad, just two hundred miles north of the grasslands. (A century later, aerial survey showed a mere four hundred elephants along the coast between Victoria and Rio del Rey.) None are found in the grasslands.

On the plateau, where the altitude ranged from 4,000 to 8,000 feet, the mountains were still volcanic, but only slightly so. They were still difficult to climb, but gentler, more undulating. A haze covered them during the harmattan, when the searing winds ripped down from the Sahara, bearing sand and dust; they turned an emerald green as the small rains recurred each spring. Then one could distinguish small landmarks fifteen miles away, and at night the air was so clear the stars shone with a special radiance and clarity.

The Germans, who pushed through to the grasslands in 1889, found a well-populated country, divided into many subtribes, some small, some welded together into large groups. The Bali and Bafut were two of the great tribes whose paramount chiefs held the power of life and death over their peoples.

The Bafut can be traced back about three or four hundred years to a large group of people called the Tikari, who had migrated into the grasslands from what is now northern Nigeria and the Sudan. They were victims of mounting pressures from slave seekers who for centuries had been supplying the slave markets of North Africa. In successive waves, the Tikari came to the grasslands, where for a time they found respite and comparative security.

Then came Fulani and Chamba warriors, horsemen from

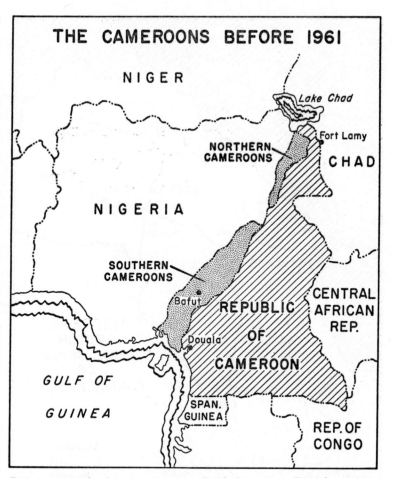

THE CAMEROONS BEFORE 1961

Before 1960, the Cameroons were divided into two British sections in the west and French Cameroon in the east, which became the Republic of Cameroon in 1960. In 1961 the former British colony split up: the people of the Northern Cameroons voted to join Nigeria; the Southern Cameroons voted to join the Cameroon Republic to form the Federal Republic of Cameroon.

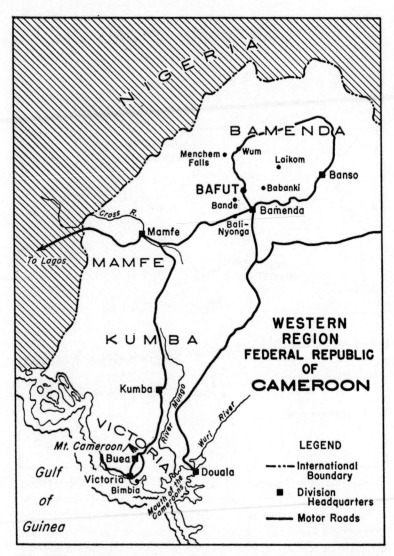

The Western Region, former British territory, comprises about one tenth of the area and one fourth of the population of Federal Republic of Cameroon.

Nigeria and the Sudan, hunting slaves both for their own use and to sell to northern traders. At first many of the Tikari tribes tried to fight them off, but without adequate weapons the battles were pitifully one-sided. Before guns became plentiful, the Tikari had fortified the town of Foumban by digging great ditches fifteen feet deep, and erecting, above these, mud walls fifteen feet high. At intervals along the wall they built lookout towers, while down in the ditches they placed sharpened poles. The mounted Fulani, attempting to scale the walls, first had to clear the ditches. Many of them fell onto the shafts, which killed or maimed the horses and many of the riders. For a time this proved successful, but wave after wave of Fulani finally succeeded in scaling the walls, killing many of the inhabitants and dragging off the rest into slavery.

To escape these depredations, many tribes fled to new territory. It is probable, too, that population pressures, famine, and internecine wars were factors in this migration, which seems to have taken place over many years, beginning as early as A.D. 1600. In the course of these movements of population, tribes mingled with other tribes. The Tikari grew until they became the largest ethnic group on the grasslands. One of these Tikari offshoots, ancestors of the present Bamum people, just east of the Bamenda plateau, may have been the forebears of the Bafut. Even today the Bafut people look upon them as their brothers. Some of them travel back to Foumban as faithful Moslems do to Mecca.

According to their own legend, when the Bafut fled from the Fulani warriors, they lived for many years on the great Ndop plain, which was then, just as it is today, a gently undulating plateau, lush with elephant grass, thick with game, and able to support a large population. When their Fon died, three of his stronger sons wrangled fiercely over which should succeed him. The argument seemed about to flare into open battle until one son suggested that they divide the tribe and that two of them move elsewhere to establish new villages.

With the help of the tribal diviner, they decided to give two quarters (or wards) of the village to the son who made the brilliant suggestion, and the other two sons would each receive one quarter. One son stayed at Ndop, the son with the two quarters moved his people over to what is now Big Babanki, and the last son moved his quarter to Mbabari, not far from the present site of Bafut village.

Here the Bafut tried to force allegiance from the neighboring tribes. This often required strong persuasion. When the nobles of one tribe would not pay tribute to Bafut, the Fon invited them to a hunt and a subsequent feast. In a hut, while the guests ate, the men of Bafut fell upon them and slaughtered most of them (the rest, discovering what was happening, escaped, abducting one of the Fon's wives in revenge). Another time, the Fon captured a neighboring subchief who had slain a leopard and had not given it to the Fon. The leopard was, and is, a sign of royalty, and is always reserved for the Fon. The chief agreed to pay tribute. Another tribe had to be disciplined by having its village burned.

With the chief of the Mbabari, there was little trouble. As chiefs went, he was not very important, and he agreed to allow the Fon of Bafut to reign over his territory, and he retired to a secondary position. He was, of course, well paid with slaves, ivory armlets, the valuable blue-and-white cloth from the Jukun tribes in the Sudan, carved drinking horns, brass pipes, and figurines.

In those days, one of the important personages in the king's household was his mother. As queen mother, she held the highest feminine position in the tribe. Her son took her advice upon many occasions, and she was treated with deference by all the people, even judging certain cases of misdemeanor among the women without help from the male councilors. She was given choice land to farm, and many presents were lavished upon her. Her commands were instantly obeyed by the Fon's wives and children.

When the tribe had been established at Mbabari for some time, the queen mother descended one day from their hill to a stream in a lush valley near the present site of Bafut. After fishing for a while, she wandered up to a level area rich in trees, with good land for farming. It was an excellent location for a settlement, she realized, and she reported this to her son. The Fon was impressed and sent four emissaries to look over the area. When they returned with a favorable report, it was decided that the entire village would move.

The people came down from Mbabari to clear the land in the valley. They built a royal compound with a central house—the Achum—for the Fon. It was a huge hut with a high grass-thatched roof. Separate huts were erected for the Fon's many wives and their children. Finally, arranging their own homes and compounds in quarters around the Fon's area, they completed the village.

In the three hundred or more years since their migration to the Bamenda grasslands, the might of the Bafut has been greatly respected, and upon occasion neighboring tribes have felt their wrath. When the Germans stalked out of the forest, the Bafut were well established, deferred to by their neighbors, and feared by those villages that had borne the brunt of their hostility.

A Casual Affair

The fondest wish of every West African woman was to have a child. In Bafut the event was not given any undue anxiety or ceremony. Women often worked out in their fields up to the time of birth. With Ashoh, however, back in—as near as can be calculated—1884, there was a difference. As a wife of the Fon, she was entitled to take extra precautions, even though she had already had several children. A week or so before the baby was due, she asked two of her co-wives to assist her in the fields. She was thinking of her sister, married to a commoner in the village, who had been alone when her baby arrived and had had to call in a neighbor at the last moment—luckily a married man who knew what to do. Any married person, in fact, could stop to give aid, and in some cases quite a few people might be present.

Ashoh had her two co-wives to help her when her child was born. In traditional Tikari fashion, they buried the afterbirth in a little hole in the floor of the hut. There was no special ceremony. Ashoh had carefully observed all the taboos of prenatal conduct: she had not eaten young stinging ants or honey; she had not chopped firewood or pounded corn fufu. Nor had she watched the juju dancers at the ceremonies, for she knew that if she gazed on a juju mask, the child would resemble it. Fortunately, she had not dreamed unwholesome fantasies; had she dreamed she was to bear twins, it would have meant that her child would be stillborn, or worse, that she would die in childbirth. Most important, she had taken the precaution of conceiving her child on the leopard-skin couch of the Fon. This would ensure, if it were a boy, that he would be eligible for the chieftainship.

Ashoh was delivered of a strong fine boy. The women rubbed mother and child with palm oil to make the skin soft, and then fed Ashoh a nourishing soup. There was no feast, no singing or dancing, though friends and relatives brought small gifts when they heard the news. As the son of a divine king, ruler over twenty thousand people and seven villages, the baby was given presents of cowrie shells and brass manillas, or bracelets, the currency of the day. Aside from that, no special note was taken of his birth.

Among the scores of offspring of the Fon, no one could know that this child would one day sit on the leopard-skin dais in the Achum as the Fon of Bafut.

Ashoh kept the baby well fed, washed, and oiled. During the first week she ate several times a day to regain her strength, but she ate alone or occasionally with one other woman or a young girl. She did not eat in the presence of a man for at least a month after the birth. Nor would she be allowed to sleep with her husband for at least two years, for until the baby was weaned, she could not risk pregnancy: the precious mother's milk was needed for the baby. At a small celebration, during that first week, the head male of Ashoh's family gave a short talk and then pronounced the boy's name: Ingwa. Had he been the first son, he would have been given his father's name or possibly that of his maternal grandfather. But Ingwa was the fifty-first child of the Fon, so he was given a fairly common Bafut name, that of a dead chief.

During the first week, too, the baby was circumcised by old Shu, whose special duty it was to perform this ceremony. A piece of fiber string was attached to the foreskin, and the skin was stretched tight and cut. The foreskin was placed in a hole of a plantain tree that grew inside the compound; when the plantains ripened, Ingwa's father, Aboumbi, would kill a fowl and call Muma, his oldest brother, to partake of it. After the cutting, the wound was rubbed with sacred leaves that the medicine doctors had mixed in a calabash of cold water. Four times a day the wound was treated in this fashion, to soften the skin and prevent cracking; after the second week it was healed. Circumcision was performed so the boy "could urinate properly"; later, it would ease sexual intercourse.

That same week the Fon came to visit Ashoh. He brought with him a sharp knife with which he shaved Ingwa's head. Later,

Ashoh kept it clean-shaven until the boy was old enough to do it himself. After these first few visits the Fon seldom came to the hut, but once in a while Ashoh carried the child into the royal yard so the chief could see how his son was progressing.

As the boy grew older he began to look more and more like his father. There was a familial resemblance among all the Fon's children, and people at the market often remarked that a certain child must surely come from the royal compound. At that time the Fon had nearly one hundred wives—not many for a land where polygyny was an ancient custom. Plural wives, however, depended somewhat on a man's economic status, so a commoner was usually restrained to a mere two or three. Noblemen and members of royalty, naturally, because of their higher economic station, often had twenty or more wives. Kings and paramount chiefs maintained wives in the hundreds. On the eastern edge of the grasslands, one Fon had around four hundred wives, and the early European explorers in East Africa found several chiefs whose wives and concubines were even more numerous. The king was the father of the tribe; he was expected to guarantee the superiority and ascendancy of his people over all others by assuring that his numerous wives would bear many children. These descendants would, in turn, mature and multiply, so that the Bafut people would become strong and mighty.

While the boy was living mainly on his mother's milk, he was also given, at about six months, such solid foods as ripe bananas, cocoyams,* and bits of meat when available. All of this food was first pulverized on a grinding stone. Around the age of two the boy was weaned, and then, while Ashoh went to her fields, he stayed in the compound in the care of an older brother.

The young children spent most of their time at rowdy games, singing, dancing, and fighting with each other. One of their favorite pastimes was greeting the Fon each morning as he came out of his house to commence his daily rounds; on these tours he inspected first the compound and then the village itself. When he appeared, the children gathered around him, begging for little tidbits of food, crying that they didn't get enough to eat. The Fon tolerated this game, and although he usually told a

* Cocoyam was the regional term for dry taro, the tuber which formed a staple of the West African diet.

wife or an enchinda to fetch some fruit or bits of meat for the babies, now and then he sharply refused them anything. This occurred when some affair of state worried him or there was trouble in an outlying village. Bafut men, as a rule, were very permissive with all children, and the Fon was no exception.

When he and his mother visited in the village, Ingwa walked, for it was important that he learn at an early age to travel long distances. Usually he was encouraged to carry something on his head; it was not at all uncommon for children of nine or ten to carry loads of forty or fifty pounds on their heads. However, while he was still quite young, if a journey with his mother was a long one, she carried him in an antelope-skin sling, even though he was a sturdy child and needed no pampering.

During those early years his mother sometimes prepared a tiny feast for him to share with his brothers and sisters. Before going to her farm in the morning, Ashoh arranged bits of meat, cocoyams, and fruit on a leaf. Ingwa invited his favorite play-mates to his hut, where they played games for a while. Then they ate the "feast" he served them. He loved teasing them by with-holding food from those on the fringe, but when they cried that they hadn't received any food, he magnanimously offered them a choice morsel of meat. Then, rocking from side to side with laughter, they shouted and screamed over their cleverness. This sort of humbugging went on all the time. Another favorite game of his childhood was tug-of-war. The children from the Fon's compound formed one team, and children from another quarter were their opponents. The rope was made of elephant grass. The flag they fought over was fashioned from a banana leaf, to be car-ried home in triumph by the victorious team.

Even when he was only three or four, Ingwa had his duties to perform. His mother insisted that he help carry water from the nearby stream and collect twigs for their store of firewood. He was also expected to pull the grass from the path that linked their mud huts to other huts in his father's compound. And some-times, like many of his half-brothers, he acted as a nursemaid to his younger sister, toting her sidesaddle on his hip, amusing her, and scrounging little nibbles of food to keep her from crying.

On a typical day, Ingwa and a friend dawdled in the village stream, slowly filling their calabashes with water. The village of

Bafut awaited the life-giving rains of spring. The planting was finished, the women's farms spread over the hillsides. Wood was gathered and stacked beside the houses and under the thatched eaves. All the rituals that would help assure a good harvest were complete.

Their calabashes full, Ingwa and his companion started up the steep path that led to the main street. Each balanced a small calabash on his head, using a coil of dried plantain leaves as a flat base. As they came to a shady road leading off the path, Ingwa's companion turned off to his home. Ingwa shuffled on toward the royal compound.

On through the village he walked and up the steep bank that led to the dance plaza before his father's compound. His path ran past small, individual compounds fenced in with high palings of natural plantings. These kept in each family's livestock of goats and chickens and excluded alien animals. At intervals, crotons, hibiscus, and strophanthus bloomed along this living fence. Palms and banana trees loomed over each home; little garden kitchens could be seen through the open fiber gate. In each compound the yards were swept clean. The huts were tall and graceful. There was one for the head man of the compound, one each for his wives and their children, and usually more huts for his sons and their families, together with extra storage buildings. The mud walls, twelve feet square and twelve feet tall, had been carefully plastered with mud over a framework of raffia palm, and the whole was crowned with a thick, cooling roof of thatched grass. When viewed from a distant mountain, the houses resembled newly sprung mushrooms after a rain.

The *thud-thud* of a skin drumhead could be heard, mingling softly with the rasping sound of yams being grated into wooden containers for the evening meal and the pounding of corn in big wooden tubs. In one yard, several old men sat, lazily talking together, smoking black, carved wooden pipes. Over in the corner of the compound, little children were dancing, kola-nut rattles tied around their ankles. They danced sedately, practicing the steps of their elders, one of the boys marking the rhythm by tapping a pebble against a larger stone.

The entire village encircled the spacious royal compound, where the Fon, his father, lived. Here was his father's house, the huge ancestral hut called the Achum. Here were various medicine and juju huts, and here the homes for the Fon's multitude of wives. In the vast plaza was a drum hut guarded by two gigantic ancestral boulders. This was the scene of all ritual ceremonies for the Bafut tribe. When five to ten thousand people thronged this plaza to do homage to their king and their ancestors, the very earth vibrated.

As Ingwa turned into the compound, the sky darkened as though someone had slowly waved a banana leaf over his head, blocking out the light. He looked up. The distant mountains were still bathed in sunshine, but over and behind him a lowering cloud suddenly released a torrent of rain. The cool water sluiced down his bare skin. He hurried over to his mother's hut, pushed aside a sliding door of palm fiber, and slipped into the house.

The boy had no idea how old he was. Time and space meant nothing to him, and not much more to his elders. Their yearly cycle was determined largely by the time it took to raise their millet, yams, maize, and beans; it was measured by the dry season, the first small rains, and finally, by the long wet period of five or six months, when the rivers turned into floods, it rained in torrents for hours at a time, and the sun could not pierce the curtain of lead. Time was measured by the big yearly dance, the week-long religious festival when the entire tribe gathered on the huge field before the royal compound for dancing, feasting, and honoring the long list of dead chiefs, with special honors reserved for the boy's father, the Fon. Time was measured by the coming and going of the moon. Space was calculated by the ground that could be covered in a day by foot, for these people had no beasts of burden, and every load of produce or trade goods from farm or market was carried on the head or back of a man, woman, or child.

When Ingwa went fishing he used a long, tapering basket trap with an opening at one end. He stepped carefully into the cool water of the stream and placed the trap's open end against a rock, hoping some fish might be hiding under it. Jarring the stone just enough to scare them, he caught the fish in his basket as they swam out; then, with his hand over the opening, he transferred them to his carrying bag. There were not many fish to be caught in this fashion, but what few he found could be dried and used as seasoning in stews. There were no lakes close to Bafut, and some of the streams were the homes of the sacred ancestors. This narrowed the fishing spots to those streams close to and in the village; because nearly everyone liked to fish, the catch was usually a slim one.

During the rainy seasons, when the streams were swollen from the heavy rains, the boys splashed and swam. Perhaps it was not swimming in the manner of boys on the coast, but they soon learned to keep their heads above water, for when one went under, the others let him thrash around until he found himself swimming. A weak one, however, was pulled out when the boys realized he wasn't going to make it on his own. Bafut children, like many other children the world over, were immune to their own level of cruelty, but this served as a toughening-up process.

By now the boy had grown to a height of around four and a half feet, but his weight had not kept up with the rest of him. He was a skinny, gangling lad with a happy-go-lucky grin. He was so black that he disappeared into the shadows at night. He tried to hold himself as straight as Chunga, his favorite half-brother, who was several years older. But when he shuffled down the path, humming a dance tune to himself, he bent forward slightly as though he were dancing. He loved to dance, and like all the Bafut children, he always took part in any dance he happened to find. The evening dances, held sometimes, in his father's house, were his particular delight. Then, with his brothers and sisters, he wriggled and writhed, shouted and yelled, happily running in and out of the dance circle. During the day he wore nothing but a fiber cord around his hips, with a leather penis sheath. Over his shoulder he carried the fiber bag to hold all his store of little-boy possessions. It hung nearly to his waist. Sometimes he filled it with cotton from the kapok tree, cotton which he sold on market day to one of the traders. In this way, like many Bafut boys, he found it possible to buy a little extra salt, which was always a great delicacy.

Hunting was another important activity in the growing-up process, for not only did it supply food, but it also served as the channel through which a boy could later enter manhood. Up to this time, Ingwa had never hunted alone—he had always gone with Chunga or a friend—but one day he decided to try his luck on his own. He knew that if he was to gain stature in the eyes of his family, particularly the Fon, he would have to bring back game he had shot with his own bow and arrow. He had practiced by rolling an orange down the village paths and shooting arrows at it.

He took his bow and the little skin quiver full of arrows he had made himself and walked down to the river. Then he climbed the rocky path on the other side, up the high rise beyond the stream, and plunged into the thick elephant grass. Over more hills he went, forgetting the distance, concentrating on finding some small animal for his arrow. Several tiny squirrels, birds, and little rodents crossed his path, but some he considered too small, and others scurried away before he could fit an arrow to the bow.

Suddenly there was a movement behind a clump of purple flowers. He stopped, motionless, wishing he had a dog to frighten the animal into the open. But he needed no dog, for the rodent, a good-sized cutting-grass, or cane rat, about a foot and a half long, sprang out directly in front of him. His arrow went through the animal's shoulder. The second arrow went through the head and killed it. Into his bag it went, and the boy started for home.

Ashoh was elated, but she merely instructed him to tell the Fon's number-one wife that he, Ingwa, had shot his first game. The Fon, himself, rewarded him with a brass manilla.* Some of the other princes had received a few cowries when they presented their first kill.

The next time Ingwa hunted, he borrowed a spear from his half-brother Chunga, and he took his dog. This was a fairly diminutive creature with short, fawn-colored hair and sharp, pointed ears. From its throat hung a small, iron bell with a narrow opening at the bottom and a tiny pebble inside. In the high grass it was hard for the hunter to see the animals, so the tinkling bell prevented him from spearing his dog by mistake. This time the boy returned with a tiny antelope, a duiker.

* In addition to beads and cowrie shells, old brass bracelets, termed manillas all along the West African coast, were used as money. They were also called slave bracelets, because certain quantities of them would purchase a slave. In the grasslands, the same brass manillas are still being melted down to fashion brass masks and figurines.

To celebrate this occasion, Ashoh prepared a miniature feast and invited the Fon and several members of her family. She took special care to invite her oldest brother, for it was he who would train Ingwa in all the Bafut customs; he would be, as it were, a second father.

Everyone brought something to the feast. Corn fufu was placed on a banana leaf, molded into a sort of doughnut with a hole in the center into which was poured a spicy palm-oil stew. As it went the rounds, each person took a bit of the bland farina-like substance between his thumb and first two fingers and dipped into the stew. Part of the roasted duiker had already been presented to the Fon; the rest was divided into small pieces, so a bit could be offered to each guest. Because the men were served first, the women and children were forced to be content with what was left. Everything was washed down with sharp, tingling palm wine.

Then the Fon arose and expressed his delight in this son who showed promise of becoming a fine hunter; he extolled the virtues of courage and virility. Ingwa received a spear from his father and from each male relative. After that day he was no longer considered a boy; he had entered his youth.

The Enchinda's Release

Days and nights in the tropics never change in their length. Bafut is only six degrees north of the equator, and its twelve hours of daylight yield abruptly to a night brilliant with moonlight or to total blackness. The stars, when they appear, flash and shimmer in a huge, black dome; they smile on familiar scenes, lending a magic never possessed by these in daylight.

The people of Bafut always hoped to reach their destination before dark. Nocturnal witches were everywhere, as were all sorts of evil spirits and goblins that could chase a man until he fell dead from exhaustion. If it was necessary to be abroad after the sun had set behind the mountains, it was wise to have a companion. On moonlit nights everyone felt safer, but even then, one did not travel alone if he could avoid it.

Ingwa and his older half-brother Chunga were hurrying into the village, one day, just as the sun disappeared. Chunga was about fourteen, twice Ingwa's age. He was the younger boy's favorite and served as his mentor in many ways. From him Ingwa was learning to hunt, and it was Chunga's voice he tried vainly to imitate, for it was low, soft, and persuasive. Instead of a leather sheath like Ingwa's, the older youth wore a tiny bit of cloth draped carelessly through a fiber cord, so that his front and rear were covered, but his hips were left entirely bare. He was tall and slender, with the lithe grace of one who is accustomed to walking many miles while carrying a heavy burden. His dark skin was free of the pockmarks so many Africans bore as a result of the dreaded smallpox; it was smooth skin and showed the care of constant oiling. Chunga was a vain lad and extremely fastidious in his toilet. Only his bare feet indicated his prowess as a walker: they were large, with thick, gray protrusions behind the heels and a gray callus covering the entire sole. His fine eyes were nearly always smiling, even during those rare moments when the rest of his face was sober. He had a high forehead, and his maternal uncle, with whom he lived, kept his dark, curly hair clipped so near the skull that from a distance he gave the impression of being clean-shaven.

Both boys were carrying gourds of palm wine on their heads. The following day there was to be a feast in the king's compound. Ashoh had told Ingwa to help Chunga bring more wine. They were carrying the last calabash now, before dark. One of Ashoh's nephews, Kimi, was to be released from his service as an enchinda. All his relatives had been invited to watch the ceremony, bring gifts, and take part in the feast. In her double position as a wife of the Fon and a relative of the young man, Ashoh was expected to help provide food and drink.

Enchindas were young servants of the Fon. The system was an old one in Bafut society, where the power lay firmly grasped in the hands of the paramount chief, or king. Many years ago, when they were still migrating from the northeast, it was felt that the role of Fon, with its divine power of life or death, needed a counterbalance. It is possible that during the reign of a despot, in the old days, the people became wary of royalty's great control over their affairs. A group of commoners, called Bukum, decided to do something about it. They were the important men of the tribe, good warriors and quarterheads (men in charge, more or less, of a ward, or quarter, of the village). Their titular head was addressed as Kweyifon, and soon the entire secret society was known by this name. It meant, literally, the "Thing of the Chief." The society was divided into a head man (the Kweyifon himself); a Council of Elders, the inner circle, which numbered from seven to twelve, depending on the village; and the rest of the Bukum. This secret society, along with the Fon, ruled the Bafut tribe. Throughout the grasslands, other Tikar groups possessed a society with much the same structure.

Actually, the Thing of the Chief was a brass gong, a double hand bell joined together at the top with a brass handle. This sacred musical instrument was carried by Kweyifon when he trotted through the village on his many errands. It was taboo for women to look on this gong. When they heard the ringing sound as Kweyifon struck it with a cotton-wrapped wooden mallet, they ducked into a nearby compound, hid behind a tree, or turned their faces to the wall. Dire consequences were sometimes reported as a result of not obeying this taboo. Women could lose their babies in childbirth, they could become horribly disfigured, or cause sickness to visit someone, or everyone, in the family.

Many of Ingwa's friends were or would become enchindas. Even at his early age he observed them performing their duties in the royal compound. The Bukum actually formed a class of noblemen who rose from the ranks of the commoners through a series of stages, services, and payments. Nearly always they commenced as enchindas, young boys about nine or ten years of age, who served the king and the Bukum. They received no pay, and they stayed for a period of around five years, although in the old days they had served as long as ten to fifteen years. The Fon had as many as eighty to a hundred enchindas serving as pipe bearers, stool bearers, even arm bearers and messengers. They collected palm wine and palm oil, kept the courtyards clean, and assisted Kweyifon in his myriad duties. They learned the properties and operation of the king's household and in this way became familiar with the affairs of the entire tribe.

It was an honor to be called upon to serve as an enchinda. A man sometimes offered his son for such service, or the Bukum could requisition a child from its father. When twins were born, if they were male, one was automatically reserved for the Fon's service. If one was male and one female, the boy eventually became an enchinda, and the girl was promised to the Fon for a wife, or reserved for training in his compound, then bestowed as largess to certain men whom the king wished to honor. The enchindas lived together in special quarters of the royal compound and were on call at all times. No women were allowed in their courtyard. Kweyifon was their mentor and overseer.

Kimi was a lighthearted lad of about fifteen when the Fon decided to release him from enchinda service. He had performed his duties faithfully for nearly five years, and several boys were eager to take his place. Kimi's mother and father, his brothers and sisters, his old grandfather, his mother's brothers, his aunts and uncles, and all of the Fon's wives and the Bukum came to the royal compound for the important ceremony that would free him from his years of servitude.

Ashoh had prepared several baskets of pounded cocoyams. She had bananas, kola nuts, and some dried meat for the stew. She was an excellent farmer and organizer, and she had plenty of food on hand at all times. In addition, she had ordered a personal gift for Kimi, a carved cow-horn drinking cup. The horn had been obtained in trade with the Fulani. Because carving was not one of the special crafts of the Bafut people, Ashoh had had this one made by a celebrated carver in Babanki, which added to its cost. The entire cup, with its representative symbols, had been blackened with earth and ashes, then polished through many rubbings. The Fon had ordered a goat prepared for slaughter and roasting. Hundreds of cowries, a Jukun cloth, and many gourds of palm wine were arranged neatly in the center of the courtyard.

When the visitors had crowded in and were sitting or standing along the walls, Aboumbi stalked out and, with arms akimbo, waited under the huge fig tree. An enchinda followed, carrying a beautifully carved stool, the sign of royalty throughout much of West Africa. This was placed directly behind the Fon, and without so much as a glance at it, he sat down heavily. Because the Fon was a divine king, he could not sit on an ordinary seat or chair; hence the necessity for numerous stools always to be in readiness and for enchindas to carry them. Just the carving of these seats kept many artisans occupied, in Babanki and other places.

Kweyifon marched into the yard, with Kimi at his heels. The lad was naked from the waist up, but from his hips to the ground a dark-red cotton skirt was draped. He was tall, with black skin pulled taut across his cheekbones and tight, curly hair clipped close to his head. He walked rather loosely, but with dignity, a slight smile on his lips and with enough seriousness in his mien to give no offense to the Fon. He sat down at one end of the line of Bukum, while Kweyifon gave a long speech in his honor. At last, when the crowd was growing restless, the Fon held up his hand and shouted in his loud, sharp voice that the speech was too long. Release the boy so he could enjoy his own feast!

The crowd hooted good-naturedly. Kweyifon scowled, but he led Kimi over to the Fon. The young man knelt down before the chief, holding his hands together. Aboumbi grinned; he liked this boy in spite of his lighthearted attitude. Dipping his fingers into a wooden bowl held by an enchinda, a bowl Kimi had often clasped, the Fon rubbed the young man's head with a red mixture of powdered camwood* and water. With a friendly, graceful speech, he thanked Kimi for his service. He told the youth to return to his family, to obey them as he had his king, and the ancestors would bless him.

The Fon raised Kimi to his feet, then motioned another enchinda to bring up the gifts. When these had been bestowed, Aboumbi indicated that his personal sign of regard for Kimi's service was a gun, with which to kill many leopards, many bush cow, and many Bafut enemies. This was a rare gift indeed, a true indication of the Fon's gratitude. Sometimes an enchinda was rewarded with a wife, but for Kimi the gun † was a far better gift.

Ammunition was hard to get and, probably, was obtainable only by pilfering or capture, so that both the gun and its ammunition were highly valued. In some tribes, membership in the men's military society was contingent upon the possession of a gun. Raiding parties were thus constantly being organized to search for guns and ammunition. A man bringing in war captives might be rewarded with a gun, the young enchindas in the chief's palace were sometimes given a gun at the close of their service. The men with guns were important and wealthy people in the community.

All through the feast that followed, one of the Bakum heated and tested his drum. Then, when the soft, black night had closed in and the feast was cleared away, he moved over near the fire

* The pounded inner bark of the barwood tree of West Africa. Many tribes use it for ritual ceremonies, painting religious objects as well as their own faces.

† Flintlocks probably reached the grasslands from the coast during the 1880's, and from the Benue River trade routes (and therefore Bornu and Nigerian areas to the north) possibly much earlier. There were the kind known as Dane guns, Danish Black guns, and Buccaneers. When the Germans reached the grasslands in 1889, the Bali-Nyonga, about thirty-five miles south of Bafut, had at least two thousand guns described as flintlocks.

and began to tap softly with his fingers. He started singing a social song known to everyone. Some of the Fon's wives brought out their rasps, wooden sticks with notches in them, against which they rubbed brass rings to add to the rhythm. The enchindas fastened on anklets of kola kernels, which clashed as they moved. Everyone sang and danced, going round and round in a huge circle, their feet thudding heavily but moving only a few inches at a time. They clapped their hands to the rhythm of the tall drum, hypnotized by the music, the wine, and the night. Ingwa and the boys his age joined the circle, singing the old songs along with the wives. The tiniest toddlers slipped in with the shuffling dancers, too, staring wide-eyed at the drummer as they jogged past him. Many of the women had tiny babies, still asleep, tied to their backs, and the delicate little heads jounced up and down as the mothers danced.

The palm wine flowed freely, and not a few of the Bukum became noisy and delirious. More than one of Kimi's female relatives slipped behind a hut with a new lover; the wives of the Fon, of course, were taboo to other men, but some of them watched with longing as the reckless couples fled from prying eyes.

Aboumbi hopped about near the drummer, backed up by a chorus of twenty or more wives, all jostling around him, shrieking and yelling his praises at the end of each song. When they sank to the ground to rest, the Fon shouted orders for more wine. It was late when he suddenly went in to bed. The boisterous merrymakers immediately started for their homes, helping Kimi carry his gifts. Their shouts and laughter echoed along the dark paths.

The Coming of the White Man

By the time Ingwa was born, around 1884, the Cameroons were already in German hands, but the Bamenda grasslands remained as sequestered as though they were on the other side of the moon.

No white man had ever appeared in Bafut, although a Bafut trader had once seen one when he traveled north to the markets of Adamawa. There he heard stories of other white men who had formerly engaged in the slave trade, but now had changed their minds about it and were trying to stamp it out. Slavery in Bafut was apparently never of any great importance as such, but with all the slave dealing that had been carried on for hundreds of years in West Africa, as well as the rest of the continent, it was inevitable that the Tikar tribes should indulge in so profitable an activity. Often slavery was a by-product of tribal warfare. Slaves were important as a means of barter, as ways of improving relations with other tribes, and in cementing treaties. In Bafut, once they were taken to live with a family, they were well treated, and often had the opportunity to buy their freedom. Their children were not considered slaves, and once a man's freedom was achieved, his entire background was ignored. Because of the rapid turnover, however, it is doubtful that many slaves had the opportunity to earn their liberty.

The Bafut trader also heard about white men who exchanged precious guns and ammunition, beads, and cotton goods for ivory, kola nuts, and palm oil. He heard of white explorers who wanted to search the rivers and mountains and deserts merely to see what lay beyond. The Bafut trader found it all very confusing—so much so that when he reported these things, the townspeople merely laughed at him. But Aboumbi and his Council refused to laugh, for they remembered how their people had been harassed and pursued by their ancient Chamba enemies. Even now, the Chamba descendants who had settled at Bali Nyonga to the south were not considered trustworthy and were regarded with a deep and abiding hatred.

In 1891 rumors about white men were rife in the grasslands, for despite the fact that no white man had come down from the north, white traders and missionaries from the coast were slowly working their way inland. Aboumbi kept repeating that he had no quarrel with them as long as they kept out of Bafut. He had heard a story about one white man who had actually talked a lesser chief into a blood pact so that one would not trick the other. The Fon grumbled that before he entered into a blood pact with anyone, the man's worth must be proved. *Ai*, murmured the Bukum, shaking their spears vigorously. Aboumbi was sitting, as usual, in the heavy shade of the gigantic fig tree, with his feet resting on a huge, uncarved ivory elephant tusk. He was surrounded by enchindas and the Council of Elders.

At this moment, one of the messengers, whose duty it was to sift the multitude of requests for an audience with the Fon, rushed into the courtyard. So agitated was he that he forgot to bend over and cup his hands before addressing his chief. He blurted out that a runner from Bande was outside with news of a white man in the town of Bali Nyonga. Aboumbi exclaimed roughly that the chief of Bali must be up to some mischief, and he ordered the runner to be ushered in. The Bukum roared their agreement.

The Bande man came in at a little trot. He was a thin, wiry fellow dressed in a fiber loincloth. Sweat was pouring from his face; his feet were covered with the thick dust of the trail. From a fiber carrying bag on his shoulder he took a small leather pouch, which he presented to Muma, the Fon's brother, who in turn handed it to the Fon. As the runner knelt before the chief, Kweyifon thrust a cup of palm wine into his hand, and the runner gulped its contents. The Bande chief sent his greetings, panted the runner. The Fon of Bafut was asked to forgive past transgressions and accept this bag of ammunition as assurance that what he was about to hear was true. Aboumbi nodded assent that the Bande chief would be forgiven—at least for the time being. Then he asked for the momentous news.

The yard was beginning to fill with people. Seeing a stranger running down the path to the Fon's compound, they had followed at his heels and were now crowding into the yard. The messenger stood quietly, catching his breath and waiting for the people to calm down. The wives and children of the Fon sidled in to hear the story. Ingwa was there, pushing as close to the front as he could; he had lost much of the chubbiness of a small boy, though he was not yet eight. Slipping and poking between the wives' legs, he managed to stand close behind Muma and hear the story. The boy never had seen anyone who came from so great a distance, though that distance could be covered in a day. The long story, interrupted with shouts of consternation and disbelief from the audience, made a deep impression on him.

A Bande man who was visiting the people in the forest near Bali—the Bande messenger related to the Bafut—heard that a white man had entered the grasslands. Anxious to see one, he entered Bali-town and found it in turmoil. Their chief, Garega, had indeed allowed a white man, Dr. Eugen Zintgraff, to stay in his village when Zintgraff had appeared out of the forest one day. Accompanied by bearers from the coast, the white man had paved his way inland with gifts and trinkets, among which were a ship's bell and some rockets. About twenty Bali warriors, armed with spears and Dane guns, went to meet him and escort him into the village. The Kweyifon, as envoy of the chief, had covered his spearhead with a sheath of black goatskin decorated with red leather bands, the symbol of peace.

The white man was given a carved stool to sit on and a fly-whisk, both important and popular items of chiefly regalia in the grasslands. The Bali men were entirely self-possessed, and they looked him straight in the eye as he gazed at them. Zintgraff announced that he came in peace and wished to talk to the chief about opening up trade between Bali and the coast. With the aid of several interpreters and the use of pidgin English,* for no one from the coast understood the Bali men, they agreed to take him to their chief.

---

* Although linguists agree that most Tikar dialects were possibly Bantu in origin, villages in the grasslands as close as twenty miles from each other often spoke languages not mutually intelligible. Along the West African coast pidgin English has been in use for about four hundred years.

Zintgraff seemed impressed by the well-organized village with its shaded paths and banana groves. When he reached the central square he was met by two thousand warriors, perfectly silent, sitting with their Dane guns and spears upright between their knees. The Fon, Garega, kept him waiting for a while, but finally he appeared wearing a dark-red gown whose ample folds increased his massiveness. He stood before his stone seat and looked intently at the white man. Suddenly, after talking to some of the interpreters, Garega grasped Zintgraff by the arm and raised it aloft.

See, he laughed to his Council of Elders, the white man's skin did not burn, and he could not possibly have come up out of the water as they declared. Then Garega called for palm wine and kola nuts and asked Zintgraff to tell him the story of his trek from the coast. He seemed to like the white man. When Zintgraff expressed a wish to visit Adamawa, "where people rode horses," Garega informed him his own father had come from that area, but the way was hard and it led through the territory of six chiefs en route. Perhaps it would be best if he, Garega, helped to buy the way for him.

Zintgraff then presented his gifts, and arrangements were made to house himself, his companions, and the carriers. He asked questions about the sources of ivory, the palm-oil trade, and the fertility and salubriousness of the country. Garega assented to his plans to build a station for the Germans nearby, on condition that when Zintgraff traveled north, some of his companions and carriers would stay in Bali as hostages. The white man then sent a message to his assistant, who had remained with the Banyang to the south.*

While the huts were being built, a rumor was brought to Garega that another white man, believed to be an Englishman, was warring in the forest area. Garega reported this to Zintgraff and suggested that if the stranger was not Zintgraff's brother (in other words, a member of his tribe), they should attack him and divide the spoils. Zintgraff was visibly disturbed at this, for he felt that no white man could feel safe under those circumstances.

---

* This message never got through, and on the coast and in Germany, meanwhile, it was believed that the expedition was lost and that Zintgraff had been killed.

When Garega saw his consternation, he offered blood brother-hood. Cuts were made on their arms and a paste of chewed kola and cubeb pepper was placed over the incisions, both men then licked off the paste, and blood from the cuts was poured into a vessel of palm wine. Each drank from the cup of wine and swore an oath of mutual protection. To break this oath meant that the transgressor's belly would swell in nine days, and he would die horribly.

While this ceremony was going on, the Bande messenger continued, Garega remarked that Zintgraff had come like a little cock to his house, and he could have easily killed the white man and taken his valuables. But since Zintgraff's arrival in Bali, Garega had seen and learned something of the fashion of the whites. Despite this, there were still many people who advised him to kill Zintgraff.

At this, Aboumbi shouted agreement. Yes, kill the white man!

But the messenger looked sadly around at the eager crowd. Garega had not only allowed Zintgraff to live, but had promised that no harm would come to him, for he felt it was better to obtain the knowledge of the whites and to retain them as friends to the lasting benefit of Bali-town than to take a short-lived advantage of them by robbery. The chief of Bande, therefore, thought it wise to tell the Fon of Bafut all this and inform him that Zintgraff was still making plans to go to Adamawa and would, no doubt, pass through both their villages. The messenger stopped speaking, then took a long drink of wine.

Aboumbi jumped to his feet; he brandished his spear ominously and asked if the Bafut warriors were frightened. No, shouted the men. Let the stranger come, they would kill him, and they waved their spears as though the enemies' heads were al-ready impaled on them. Tell that to the chief of Bande, ordered the Fon. Then he turned on his heel and stalked into his house. The messenger sat answering questions the rest of the afternoon. He spent the night in the military society house and the next day returned to Bande.

Bafut, however, did not settle down quickly or easily. The military society held a palaver far into the night. Many of the men also belonged to the Bukum, and the royalty were all members of Chung, another important secret society, so when they carried their decision to the Fon in the morning, it was the considered opinion of the majority in Bafut that the white man would receive no such easy treatment in their village.

The Fon smiled faintly when he heard this. He, too, had given serious thought to the matter. He had consulted late into the night with his dead father and the other dead chiefs. He had no intention of taking orders from any outsider or of being forced to pay unwarranted tribute or even hospitality.

They had not long to wait. Within weeks the runner from Bande came again with news that Zintgraff was even then marching into Bafut. Aboumbi sounded the signal drum for the military society, all of whom had been warned to be ready to march at a moment's notice. Nearly two thousand of them gathered silently in the great square outside the royal compound, some with dane guns, all of them with spears glistening in the hot sunlight.

Muma emerged from the compound and informed them that the white man was outside the village. Kweyifon had taken twenty warriors to escort the white man. The people were warned not to sell food to the stranger or to any of his carriers; without supplies they would be forced to march on. The men murmured *ai, ai,* and on the edge of the seething crowd the women echoed their assent.

Just then Kweyifon's jingling spear was heard, and the crowd became quiet again. On the path from the river they could see a long column of men bearing loads on their heads. Leading the procession was Kweyifon, followed closely by four members of the military society dressed in their warrior costumes. The white man, Zintgraff, wore a sun helmet, khaki shorts, and a cotton shirt. He was not tall, but he was very erect, and he gazed at the crowd of Africans through eyeglasses. None of them had ever seen such a contraption before. Later, Aboumbi remarked they gave him the appearance of a leopard.

As Kweyifon led the white man to a stool, the crowd pressed forward to get a better look at him. His carriers laid their burdens in a pile, then seated themselves around him; the gifts he had brought were laid out on cotton cloths in the dusty square. No one spoke. Kweyifon had disappeared into the compound. Several hours passed, and in the hot sunshine the white man was visibly nervous. His shirt was dark with sweat, and he kept fingering the brim of his helmet. Having to wait so long for an audience should have signified trouble to him, but he was determined to remain calm.

Presently ten enchindas ran out of the compound door and laid down a huge leopard skin, on which they arranged three finely carved stools. The door opened again and Aboumbi stalked out. Three times the crowd clapped and the surrounding mountains reverberated with the echoes.

The Fon was dressed in a close-fitting shirt of blue beads, with a red loincloth nearly fourteen feet long; this train he held up against his body, and in the other hand he grasped an intricately carved bush-cow horn filled with palm wine. He stood disdainfully in the sunlight, to be described later by Zintgraff as "the picture of an African despot such as I had not ever seen before or was ever to see again."

Zintgraff arose and walked toward Aboumbi, holding out his hand. At this moment Muma started to take the cup from Aboumbi, but Zintgraff grasped it first. Bewildered and angered at such poor manners, Muma asked harshly, who was the chief here?

Aboumbi told him to relinquish the horn, that because the white man had received his teachings from Garega, he could scarcely be expected to know that one did not take anything directly from the hands of a chief. Zintgraff gave them all a merry smile, and with a hearty "Prosit," drank the health of both of them. Then he went back to his stool and through his interpreter presented his gifts and his plans for the journey to the north.

Meanwhile Aboumbi, Muma, Kweyifon, and other important men were served with wine by four royal wives and the enchindas. The king ordered food to be given the carriers, and half a dozen calabashes of palm wine were set out. Zintgraff and his men, somewhat disappointed at the amount, said nothing. Finally they were led to the military society house to spend the night.

There followed a lot of sparring between the white man and the African chief. Zintgraff insisted on calling the Fon Gwalem, apparently his interpretation of the Bali name for Aboumbi, who seemed to take it in stride. Their talks were held in the Fon's palace, the Achum, a building that impressed the German a great deal. He later described it in detail: a tall house of bamboo with wooden pillars set on a platform of rocky basalt and topped with a graceful, pointed roof of thatched grass. The hall itself was a long room, open on one side, with a floor tastefully decorated with cowries.

Aboumbi lounged on a sofalike bed of bamboo covered with leopard skins, his drinking horn in his hand. A dozen or so Bukum and princes squatted around him. Zintgraff was led to a small carved stool in the corner, and his interpreter sat half out of the hall on the open side. Quantities of palm wine were constantly being consumed by everyone, and apparently Zintgraff kept up his end, no doubt hoping that provisions for his carriers would be forthcoming; he had found it difficult to buy food, for few of the villagers would deliberately disobey the Fon's order. Every morning while he talked with the Fon, one of the slaves (probably an enchinda) appeared with a round-bellied pot filled with cooked beans and cocoyams, and from every conceivable corner the naked little children of the Fon rushed forth with outstretched hands.

During the talks, Zintgraff learned from some of his men that nearby chieftains were coming and going, and he was afraid that hostilities were imminent. He presented Aboumbi with more and more presents, gifts that Aboumbi considered niggardly but that Zintgraff considered uncommonly numerous and expensive. Finally, however, arrangements were completed.

At this point, a man appeared outside the Fon's house with a cooking pot and called to Zintgraff's followers to come and eat someplace around the corner. The white man was left alone with Aboumbi and the Council of Elders. Zintgraff, for comfort, had put on a roomy burnoose, or gown, and was carrying no arms. Several of the Bukum went up to feel his skin, and one of them tried to take off his glasses, but Zintgraff, angered at what he considered an assault on his person, managed to keep them intact.

Aboumbi, meanwhile, lay back on his couch, grinning at the white man's discomfort. Finally, he ordered his men to desist, and they went in to the other room.

A few minutes later Zintgraff's companions returned. The Fon explained, through the interpreter, that his men merely wanted to feel the white man's skin and to inspect his eyepiece. The German haughtily remarked that it was not necessary for the Fon to think he had been alarmed, that the Fon was indeed a fool to think he could frighten a white man in this way. And to leave no doubt, he repeated this in Bali language. But Aboumbi blandly replied that nothing had been further from his mind, and they drank more palm wine until nightfall.

At dawn the next morning the expedition was ready to leave. Zintgraff went to Aboumbi's private courtyard once more, where he received four enchindas to act as guides on the trip. He didn't trust the Fon, however, for he asked him as a parting gesture to mix blood with him. Aboumbi became indignant at this and arrogantly refused; but he did share a kola nut and pepper with the white man, stating this must suffice as a sign of honesty. Although Zintgraff was well aware that the Bafut and the Bali Nyonga were enemies, he seemed to think it strange that Aboumbi refused to mix blood with a man who had already mixed with Garega's blood. As he marched out of the compound and down the village path, Aboumbi shouted angrily that he hoped never to see him again.

It was thought by some observers that old Aboumbi was doing a heavy trade in slaves with the markets to the north, and this was one reason he had treated Zintgraff in so surly a fashion—he was trying to keep the white man from prying into his business affairs. If this was true, Aboumbi had shunted the German aside merely because he already had more competitors for his wares than he needed. The Fon was totally ignorant of the power play going on in Europe, where the major governments had sliced the map of the African continent into convenient pieces of colonial territories. Zintgraff, on the other hand, was not sure exactly where the German autonomy ended (border lines were hard to establish in the unexplored territory), and he was sincere in attempting to open up the area for trade. He had been led to believe, probably by the Fon of Bali, that the Bafut chief held great stores of ivory, and he meant to get it.

Not long after Zintgraff left for the north, the Fon and Kweyifon called the Bukum together to discuss the possibilities of the German's return. He might pass through their village on his way back from Adamawa; he might bypass the village but send messengers in to ask for provisions; he might ignore Bafut entirely, although no one gave this much consideration. The Fon had treated the white man as civilly as he felt necessary, but he still harbored a feeling of foreboding.

The military society held nightly meetings to perfect their plans for an emergency; the air was filled with drummings and singings. Messengers were constantly on the go between the Bande, Bafut, and other subtribes who were their brothers against the Bali. Aboumbi reasoned that if Garega was now a blood brother of the white man, he would soon have to fight for his new friend. Food was gathered and stored against a possible siege. The women took their younger sons to the farms to watch for strangers on the roads; families living in outlying compounds checked their friends and relatives in the village, anyone with whom they could live in case of hostilities.

The Fon went often to his inner room to commune with his dead father. He described what had happened and begged his father to give a sign, some manifestation, of how to handle this situation. He sent Kweyifon to the diviner for advice. The Council of Elders made an unscheduled trip to the sacred pool at Menchem waterfall, where other dead chiefs resided. Here they slit the throat of a slave and threw him into the swirling water; he was followed by a calabash of palm wine, and then Kweyifon begged for assistance and counsel to meet this new threat. One of the medicine societies mixed a special potion to place on grass ropes; these were laid across each path leading into Bafut. The potion was similar to the medicine used to keep witches out during the spring of the year, when high winds brought disease and sickness. The signal drum in the plaza boomed often during those weeks, calling the men to various meetings and battle practice.

Young as he was, Ingwa joined with his age group in practicing for battle. The boys carried sticks on their shoulders, emulating their fathers and older brothers. The military societies worked with spears and a few guns until they all felt invincible, not only against the Bali men, but against any white man who might appear.

Some months later, two Bali men accompanied by two African strangers walked into Bafut. Aboumbi then learned that

Zintgraff had returned to Bali and sent these messengers to ask for thirty oxen as payment for the presents Zintgraff had given on his trip north. The Fon became indignant at this and roared that he would send one ox to Zintgraff and no more; even this was too much for the poor gifts he had received. At the time Zintgraff left Bafut he had not trusted the guides lent him by the Fon, and getting them drunk one day, he slipped away; this, too, Aboumbi considered an insult. According to Zintgraff the guides had deliberately misled him, so he felt he had to evade them.

Zintgraff's mind, however, was on the ivory he felt sure was hidden in Bafut. He stayed in Bali for a while, helping to mend the huts set up for the German station. Then, still on excellent terms with Garega, he left for the coast. He was gone for over two years, during which time he visited Germany.

During the two years of Zintgraff's absence the usual skirmishing went on among the grassland tribes. When he came back once more to Bali, he realized that the warfare among the tribes would have to be stopped if there was to be any time and energy left for trading. He was determined to open up trade relations in the grasslands so that all the caravans could be funneled along a peaceful and secure route to the coast. Also, he was beginning to recruit workers for the coastal area; some of the Bali, as well as people of the forest area, went to Victoria and Douala to work on the plantations.

Garega, all this time, had seemed to embrace the interests of his white friend; possibly he saw himself as the ultimate leader of the entire grasslands, and he surely realized the economic opportunities offered by commerce with the coast.

Because of Garega's insistance that Bafut had much ivory, a trading expedition was sent to the Bande and Bafut. The Bande chief received the traders in a diffident manner; he was not overly fond of Garega, but he had to stay on friendly terms with him. At the same time, he found it expedient to remain allied to the Fon of Bafut. He promptly sent a runner to Aboumbi, informing him of the approaching Bali messengers. The Fon sent a small delegation to the outskirts of the village to escort the men into the royal compound.

There were only four: two Bali men and two strangers—Vai men from Liberia, whom Zintgraff had recruited on his return from Germany. He had fortified his position in Bali by bringing in four hundred Vai carriers and several Europeans, all of whom had previous experience in West Africa.

When the Fon heard this, he shouted that they were not afraid of any Bali, or any Vai, or any Europeans! What did the German want?

The Bali men answered that because the Fon had refused to show Zintgraff the way north, the German now demanded from the Fon five elephant tusks, five leopard skins, and five women. At this the Fon leaped to his feet and brandished his spear at the spokesman. One of the Vai messengers then showed him a clip of cartridges and said that if the Fon did not accede to their request, war would come. But the Fon angrily motioned to several warriors who were acting as bodyguards; they immediately seized all four men and dragged them off to one of the huts in the rear. That night the Vai men were killed and their heads thrust upon the gateposts outside the royal compound. The Bali men were set free in the morning and ordered to return to their camp at Bande before they, too, were decorating a gatepost.

Zintgraff considered this an act of aggression that must be avenged. When he heard that the Bande and Bafut chiefs had put down magic on the roads leading to their villages, he sent young Bali boys to relieve themselves on it; it was a trick he learned from the Africans themselves. War was inevitable.

Before setting out, Zintgraff wrote the governor in Douala for reserves and munitions to be sent to Banyang. A new governor, however, was now in charge, and he did not consider the Zintgraff expedition an activity of the German Cameroons colony. He did not even deign to answer the letter. However, Aboumbi and his Bande ally were unaware of this, and they proceeded with their plans to defend their way of life and destroy their enemy. They knew the Bali warriors and the Germans would pick up allies wherever they could, but the Bande and Bafut had their own confederates who were eager to help. It was decided to make a stand outside of Bande, in territory that both knew well and that was accessible to friends so that provisions could be brought up when needed—but that was also hilly and forested enough to prove embarrassing to the foe.

The Bafut warriors arrived in Bande in time to spend the

night, for their spies had warned them that Zintgraff and Garega were close to the village. Early in the morning, while the women and youths stayed behind to protect the food and bring ammunition if needed, the men walked out to the first low ridge of hills beyond the town. There were about five thousand of them—strong, black, naked men, some with narrow leather loincloths and fiber bags to hold their ammunition, some with the longer trains of the military elite, and some wearing gigantic circular headdresses of chicken feathers. They had painted their bodies and faces with meaningful designs in red camwood and white lime or ashes. Because the Bali, also, wore battle designs, it was a weird and spectacular throng that appeared in the morning sunlight.

As the German, his six European aides, the Vai carriers (who had been persuaded to fight by promises of extra pay), and the two thousand or so Bali warriors advanced on Bande, one of the Vai men foolishly let off his carbine, announcing their approach too soon. The Bande and Bafut men rushed to meet them, carrying a white flag that signified battle; they had destroyed the German flag Zintgraff had sent as a gesture of friendship. Soon the warriors were in the thick of the action, shouting for the blood of their enemies and calling on their ancestors for strength.

Kimi and his young friends had been told to stay in the rear, to watch the rear lines and bring up ammunition and spears as needed. But Kimi abruptly found himself next to Muma, who was loading his dane gun and preparing to run forward in the next charge. Muma grinned at the youth; the older man was hugely enjoying this battle with the ancient enemy. Then he saw a white man ahead of him. He motioned to Kimi to help him close in. There were four of the white men, fighting valiantly.

Muma forged ahead and shot one through the chest; another was about to fire in return when Kimi lunged at him with his spear, pinning him to the ground. His horrible screams and the naked, black warriors advancing unnerved the two remaining white men, who probably feared being taken prisoner. They turned to each other and, shouting and gesticulating, shot themselves through their heads. A Bali man who had watched all this went plunging to his rear lines to report to Zintgraff. That gentleman, however, was nowhere to be seen, for he had observed smoke coming from the Bande village and, believing the battle won, had returned to Bali. But the fire had been started when one of the Bafut men set off his dane gun; sparks had set fire to the thatched roof.

The Bali soldiers, Vai carriers, and remaining Europeans were finally routed and harried all the way back to Bali. Then the victors turned their energies to helping the boys and women put out the Bande fire. After attending their wounds and counting their dead, the Bafut returned home, taking with them as many heads as they could carry, for these were important trophies of war; they were the prizes that would enable them to receive the coveted red feather from the Fon, and the jaws of the dead enemies would decorate the war drums "like little flowers." A few prisoners had been taken, and as their first deeds of slavery they were set to work helping carry the spoils back to the village.

In the old days the cessation of intertribal hostilities was sometimes marked by a blood covenant between the two chiefs concerned. Each chief traveled in turn to the territory of the other, sometimes performing the ritual at the border. In one instance, the chief of Bafut, accompanied by his retinue of elders and enchindas, military men and medicine men, went to the compound of his former enemy. There, after a proper exchange of gifts, medicine was prepared and placed in the mouths of two sacrificial slaves; their throats were then cut, and they were buried. This medicine was so potent that it would instantly affect any Bafut man or his former enemy had he attempted to recommence hostilities. Then small incisions were made in the wrists of the two chiefs. A small amount of blood was drawn from each wound and poured into a cup of palm wine. Each chief, in turn, drank from the cup.

Because the trouble with Bali had been instigated primarily by the white man, Aboumbi did not enter into a peace treaty with the enemy. Instead, both the Bande and Bafut tribes held stupendous celebrations, congratulating themselves on routing the white man. The rejoicing went on for weeks, and had the Germans returned immediately with their Bali minions to the scene of their defeat, they would have been opposed by a mere handful of boys and a few women. The entire population was on a spree that was to last, literally, until all the available palm wine was gone.

Every night there was a feast in the royal compound, beginning with the presentation of trophy heads taken in battle. After the grisly things were hoisted up on the compound wall for the whole village to gloat over, the Fon presented each warrior with the coveted red feather. This feather, which is still worn today in the Cameroon cap, was always awarded to any man who killed a bush cow, a leopard, or a man. It was obtained from the wing of one of the plantain eaters, the touraco. This lovely bird, the size of a crow, was called the "crown bird" by early Europeans in West Africa, because the top of its head extended upward into a crown. Behind the eye was a brilliant white streak, but it was the crimson crown and the wing quills that were sought for battle trophies. The rest of the bird's plumage was a rich, glossy purple.

Not to wear the red feather, once it had been awarded, was considered an affront to the chief.

Kimi, of course, with the affirmation of Muma, received several red feathers. As Ingwa and the other small boys looked on, Kimi placed them carefully in his woven cap and, with a grin, stuck it at a jaunty angle on the back of his head.

The Red Feather

Young Ingwa had watched the fighting with the Germans from a safe distance. Specific orders were issued that no chances were to be taken with several of the Fon's sons, Ingwa and his older half-brother Chunga among them. From a distant hill they observed the battle. When the fire broke out and the Bali warriors and Germans retreated southward, Ingwa and Chunga were allowed to help fight the fire.

By 1900 the grasslands were again relatively quiet. The Bafut people carried on their traditional ways, as well as trading with their neighbors one month and skirmishing with them the next. Because he still lived in the palace compound, Ingwa observed the activities that occurred each day. Already he was familiar with much of Bafut culture. At about sixteen, therefore, he was deemed mature enough to join the royal secret society known as Chung.

As the Bukum exercised their power through helping the Fon govern the Bafut people, another controlling body, Chung, wielded its influence in a more oblique way. It was composed entirely of young princes, sons and brothers of the king. This, like some of the other societies, was a military group as well as a ritualistic club that attended to the vital needs of the tribe. Chung was particularly concerned with the funeral arrangements of its royal members and their families. Bafut was an ancestor-worshiping tribe, and so this was a significant and powerful group.

Ingwa now was close to six feet tall, loose-limbed and slender, but strong and well aware of his position as a son of the Fon. He no longer lived in his mother's hut. He spent each night in the royal compound still, but in a house set aside for adolescent boys. It was the custom, and still is, to have all the royal sons, until they are around eighteen years old, spend their nights in this special hut. However, the boys still took their meals with their mothers, younger brothers, and sisters.

Chunga had left the compound several years before and was living in the village with his maternal uncle. He came to Ingwa one night just as the swift dusk was falling and a full moon was bursting over the hills. He told Ingwa to come with him to the meeting of Chung. The younger prince rose, picked up his spear, and soundlessly followed his half-brother from the compound. On the village path, they whispered together as they hurried along, hardly aware of the early night noises, the palm leaves moving slightly in a soft breeze, a kingfisher's last screech before settling down for the night, the frogs croaking down in the hollows near the stream. Nor did they mark the reflection of a huge ghost-colored bell of pale strophanthus in its dark cloud of foliage.

When they entered the compound, Ingwa, with the aid of the moonlight and the firelight, saw many of his older half-brothers, uncles, and men more distantly related. It happened that he was the only novice present, and for this reason he sat down, humbly waiting to be recognized. The Fon was not present; upon becoming Fon, Aboumbi ceased to be a working member of Chung, although his brother, Muma, always relayed progress reports of the meetings.

The men finished their discussion before Muma turned to Chunga and asked who was with him. Muma was well acquainted with the boy and Chunga knew it, but he dutifully explained that it was Ingwa, fifty-first child of Aboumbi. He was a good hunter and fighter, a boy with a sense of honor and a sense of duty. Some of the older princes had suggested he be summoned.

It was a severe look the youngster received from his uncle. Muma was second in command in the entire tribe; it was he who sat at the left hand of Aboumbi, his council that was sought on all important issues. He was a tall, husky fellow with dark, shiny skin and luminous eyes. He wore a cotton gown that fell straight from his shoulders to his ankles. He always bore himself with an air of deliberate assurance, although upon occasions such as this he could unbend a little to make the boy feel more at ease.

In his thin, sharp voice, Muma recounted what he knew of Ingwa's courage and ability as a hunter and warrior. Ashoh's family had indicated a willingness to pay for his initiation into Chung, but, in addition, the boy must accompany the older men on the morning hunt for a leopard that had been reported in a nearby valley. For the rest of the night the men sat talking in low voices, reminiscing about other hunts and planning this one.

When Ingwa returned to his hut he knew exactly what his role would be. He knew that his uncles had promised to pay five goats, fifty large colored beads, and four gourds of palm wine as his initiation fee. In compensation, he would be expected to reimburse some of this as he grew older and rose in economic status and prestige.

In the morning, while the eastern sky was just beginning to brighten and before the villagers were up, Chunga came again to escort him to the compound. The hunters had already gathered. Because this was an initiatory hunt, none of the commoners were taking part; but the early risers laughed mockingly as the men and youths filed down the village path toward the forest.

Ingwa knew this derision was directed at him, and he shouted insults back to them. His fellow hunters smiled approvingly. It was not good Bafut form to receive abuse in silence. Every man was naked, except for a bark loincloth. Each one carried a spear, many of the older men had hunting dogs with them, and all the more important men had guns.

Because this was Ingwa's first hunt with older men, he was not expected to outshine them. However, he was aware that he was being watched closely by his uncles and half-brothers. He was determined to perform as well as he could, and when at last they discovered the leopard and closed in for the kill, he was very nearly mauled as he came too near the wounded beast.

Among the Bafut and other Tikar tribes, the ferocious leopard was granted a healthy respect, and in addition, it was considered sacred and inviolate. Only the Fon was permitted to possess a leopard skin, although, at certain ceremonies, all the royal males wore a tiny bit of leopard skin around their loins. The beast was regarded as a Fon in disguise, and sometimes, when the hunters saw one in the forest, it seemed to them that the animal "opened his face to show himself to be a Fon." When this happened, the hunters refused to shoot but kept searching for a leopard that might be a Fon from another area, and therefore safe to kill.

Ingwa had displayed the requisite aggressiveness, bravery, and tenacity. His uncles were well pleased. The exhilaration of the chase stayed with him long after they returned to the royal compound. He twisted fretfully as he sat with the hunters and waited for his father to emerge and examine the trophy.

In his sharp, grating voice, Muma described to the Fon Ingwa's behavior on this, his first, leopard hunt. The Fon received the news with no outward show of emotion; his sons were expected to comport themselves with courage and aggressiveness. He asked pertinent questions, however, questions that revealed how well he recalled the thrills and hardships of the hunt. Obviously he was satisfied with the answers.

The townspeople were not present at this ceremony, only the members of Chung. It was here that Ingwa's further initiation would continue during the night. When his brother finished, the Fon sent one of the enchindas into his private quarters. The lad emerged carrying an exquisite, full-length cotton gown, heavily embroidered with traditional Cameroons emblems: the lizard, the double-gong, and the spider, emblems considered to bring good luck, good health, and long life to the wearer.

As Ingwa was pushed forward by his companions to receive his prize, Aboumbi boomed that this was his reward for bravery in his initiatory hunt. Before his peers Ingwa received his reward. He was humble as he knelt before the Fon, but then his face relaxed into a fleeting smile as he murmured his thanks through cupped hands.

Dancing, feasting, and drinking went on far into the night. Even the royal children, hanging about like puppies on the fringe of the excitement, managed to consume their share of wine. When the Fon went into his house, the noise ceased abruptly. As most of the crowd disappeared to their homes, Ingwa was escorted into a little palm hut where some of the former chiefs were buried. Although he had lived all his life in the compound, he had never entered this hut, but he knew its purpose. With Chunga still at his side, he was ordered to wait until summoned.

Desperately he wanted to ask Chunga what was about to happen, but he knew that this, too, was a part of the initiation; this was a test of his endurance, to see how long he could wait silently, even after a day in the forest and a night of dancing. The two youths sat in the darkness, neither of them speaking; only their thoughts and the dead chiefs kept them company. Moonlight, which was beginning to fade now, came in through the open door. Ingwa knew that morning was near, for the moon was about to drop behind the black mountains in the west. He heard the tremulous, mournful sound of an owl in the distance and, closer, the sibilant palm leaves moving slightly in the breeze.

A dark figure stepped through the doorway. A voice they did not recognize ordered them to rise. The boys followed their guide to another house, where other dead chiefs were buried. Here, a fire was burning in the center of the room, and to one side, a bamboo pipe protruded from the ground. This was the tube down which libations of wine were poured to the dead chiefs. Usually it was covered with a stone, a sacred flute, horns, and animal bones.

Muma, Ingwa's teacher from then on, motioned them both to be seated on the two little wooden stools directly in front of him. The rest of the night, Muma and his assistants, old Shu, who had circumcised the boys, and Ndi, the oldest uncle of the Fon, repeated the history of the society. Chunga knew most of it, for he had passed his initiation, but Ingwa sat far into the morning trying to repeat accurately what he heard.

For seven nights he was instructed in the complexities of the society, its ceremonies, its songs. The eighth day, instead of returning to his hut to rest, he was taken to the medicine hut. Several old medicine men were there, some sitting around talking, a few with iron knives in their hands. Now Ingwa would receive his cuts, the markings that indicated he had become a member of Chung. As his uncle spoke, Ingwa saw Aboumbi come out of the palace, and he dared not cry out or reflect pain in any way. A Bafut warrior, who could inflict the harshest cruelty on others, was expected to sustain his own physical pain with a proud self-assurance. The hauteur Zintgraff had observed in Aboumbi was molded, partially, in the Chung society; it was learned at an early age from the elders of the tribe, and was inculcated into all Bafut males through years of fighting other grassland peoples and nearly always emerging the victors. The Fon sauntered over to the medicine hut and talked briefly with the men who were preparing for the scarification. Then he left the compound.

A strong potion was given the boy, one that would deaden his senses just enough to enable him to bear the pain. Leaves were dipped out of the gourd where they had been soaking, sacred leaves used in many ceremonial and medicinal rituals. They would soothe the wounds. When all was ready, Ingwa was laid on his back on a fiber mat. The two older men knelt on either side and grasped his arms and thighs. The cuts were made quickly. They were arranged on his chest in the prescribed pattern for a son of the Fon. Old Shu did the work; he cut skillfully, and when it was over, Muma himself took the calabash of medicine and gently poured it over the youth's chest. Bleeding profusely, Ingwa was pulled to his feet by Shu, Ndi, and Chunga and helped into a medicine hut. Here he was given more palm wine with a sedative in it. Finally he drifted off to sleep, while old Muma and Ndi kept watch. He was, at last, a member of the royal society of Chung.*

When Ingwa shot his first leopard he was with two other youths, his half-brother Neba and Kimi, the former enchinda who so distinguished himself in the battle with the Germans. Ingwa had endured a lot of teasing from his friends and brothers; he decided that if he were to fulfill his uncles' expectations of him as a hunter and win the red feather, he must kill either a bush cow or a leopard. He talked to Neba and Kimi about it, and they agreed to go hunting. Only Kimi had shot a leopard before this, although the other two had been in hunting parties that brought one back. Ingwa carried the flintlock gun his father had given him after the initiation. Neba and Kimi, too, carried guns, weapons they had earned in the Bafut fashion. Neba had received his when he brought back a slave from a battle with one of the forest tribes. Kimi, of course, had earned his through his service as an enchinda.

In a nearby village, a farm woman told them she had seen a leopard skulking in the bush near her farm plot. Leopards were bird and monkey eaters, and they sometimes preyed on the villagers' goats and chickens, too. She was afraid it might return.

---

* In much of West Africa, a "bush" school was held for the boys' puberty rites, during which time all the boys of that particular age group were instructed, not only in secret rituals of the tribe, but often circumcised and given details about sex. Sometime during the reign of Aboumbi, for reasons that were never given, the old Fon decided to discard the bush school in his area.

When Ingwa proposed they try to find it, she willingly showed them where she had seen it. The three youths stayed in the village that night, and early the next morning, soon after the sun began to burn the dew from the heavy grass, they started out.

They had no trouble finding the distinctive tracks that led from a small stream up to a young fig tree. Ingwa looked up and saw the leopard draped over one of the lower branches. Apparently it had eaten well during the night and was resting quietly, with just a few slight twitches of its whiskers. Simultaneously the cat smelled something wrong and opened its green eyes. Ingwa aimed for the front paw and then fired a blast that brought the animal snarling and tumbling to the ground. He knew the leopard needed its legs to climb, and he wanted it on the ground so he could follow it more easily as it limped away.

Neba and Kimi had already climbed into a tree, and before Ingwa reloaded his gun he, too, shinnied up the first tree he saw. He asked Neba to go back to Bafut and have their father send help to trail the wounded beast. Ingwa and Kimi, meanwhile, tried to follow it through the underbrush. It was hot, grim work, for the way led over low hills with red soil thickly covered by elephant grass. This was extremely dangerous, for in the high grass the angry leopard could easily jump them. More than one Bafut hunter had been mauled and killed by one of these vicious animals as it circled back, making no sound, and caught him unawares.

Neba returned with twenty hunters, seasoned veterans who knew how to track. With their help the quarry was found, lying behind a tall acacia tree several miles from where Ingwa had shot it. It was badly wounded and soon, undoubtedly, would have died from loss of blood. Ingwa killed it immediately. Then, from a safe distance, the men threw sticks at it, until they were sure it was dead. A special man had been appointed by the Fon to slit the leopard's throat, and when that was done, they trussed it up on a long pole with the feet tied together. With two men at the front and two at the rear, the leopard was carried back to the village. Whooping and yelling exuberantly, the string of hunters marched behind their trophy.

Small children joined the procession and began to sing; someone brought out a reed pipe and a gourd rattle. It was a hilarious crowd that swarmed into the palace compound, eager to

The royal compound in Bafut is impressive for its neatness and order. Achirimbi's house is at extreme left; the tall building, left center, is the memorial "Achum" to the former Fon. Also within the compound are buildings for receptions, medicine, and storage. Wives' houses are to right and left, not shown in the picture.

Wearing tribal robes and an elephant-tail headdress, Achirimbi II, Fon of Bafut, poses with a favorite wife. As monarch of twenty thousand tribesmen, he has witnessed dramatic changes in the Cameroons—from German to French and English rule, and finally, in 1961, to independence.

Achirimbi visited Lagos, Nigeria, in 1956. There he presented Queen Elizabeth with a tribute from his people: an elephant tusk, ornately carved with the sacred symbols of the Cameroons. The Queen accepted the gift, then returned it to the people of her territory.

NIGERIAN INFORMATION SERVICE

One of the most modern conveniences in Bafut is the Fon's Land-Rover, which he keeps in a garage behind the resthouse. While he was a representative in the House of Chiefs, he traveled frequently to the capital at Buea. The four-wheel drive is almost a necessity for Bafut's rough roads. Less convenient is the battered-up Dodge truck on the right: it no longer runs.

t's reputation for hospitality is well known in the Cameroons.
Fon's resthouse, where the author and her husband stayed, has
me a favorite stopover for tourists. In spite of its modern
.arance, the house, like all others in Bafut, has no electricity.
.ever, it does boast maid service by the royal wives.

Bafut babies are well cared for by their mothers. Here, a baby rides
in an antelope sling on the mother's back.

ren learn to walk long distances at an early age, often with
loads on their heads. Left, a child wears the fiber carrying
f the grasslands over his shoulder and carries a bag of salt on
ad.

A group of children with a mankala gambling board. The younger
children spend most of their time playing games, dancing, singing,
and—of course—fighting with each other.

ay-to-day care of children is the duty of older brothers and
. Here two toddlers are treated to a "sled" ride in a wooden

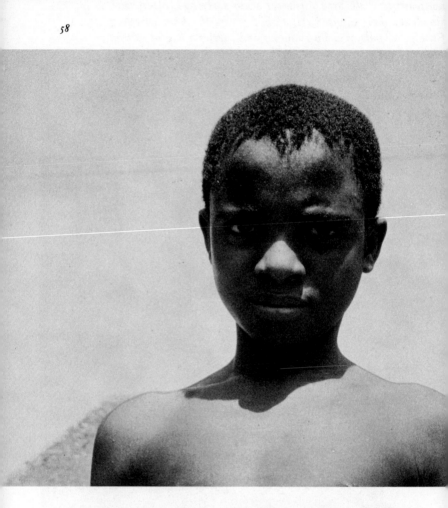

Portrait of a son of the Fon. The oldest will not necessarily be the next ruler of Bafut. By tribal tradition, Achirimbi, with the help of the Council of Elders, will probably choose his successor from among his favorite sons.

A secret society called the Bukum limits the power of the Fon and shares in the ruling of the tribe. Here, one of the elders of the society wears the secret society headdress, the Cameroons beaded necklace, and the Cameroons gown.

Their faces hidden behind hooded masks, secret society "ju-ju" men dance at funerals and other tribal ceremonies. The dancer below wears a carved mask on top of his head. Above, the head-dresses are chicken feathers attached to fiber crowns. Gowns are of cotton; anklets, of dried palm nuts.

Magic men of the grasslands. Above, a rain stopper waves a stick to drive away rain clouds during a ceremony. Below, a diviner sits with his equipment carefully spread out in front of him.

Evil witches who fly on the high winds of spring are thought to bring sickness to the community. To keep them out, a fetish, consisting of magic medicine, hangs across the road at the entrance to to the village.

Widows of the dead chief shave their heads, cover their bodies with ashes, and appear completely nude at the funeral. Joined by the chief's sisters, who keep their hair and wear fiber skirts, they join hands and parade around the field.

Women assist the wives, sisters, and daughters of a dead chief in a wailing song to his memory. In the background secret society members dance and shoot their guns for all to hear. Elaborate funeral gatherings not only honor the dead, but also bring good luck and prosperity to his descendents.

Not a time for mourning only. Believing that "life" is the greatest good, the people of West Africa rejoice when a person has lived to an old age. Dancing, singing, and even humor are parts of the funeral celebration. The dancers above clown for the camera by holding palm leaves between their teeth.

*Partially buried in the ground, this pit violin will be used to ac-
company singing. An arched stick at the top holds the string under
tension.*

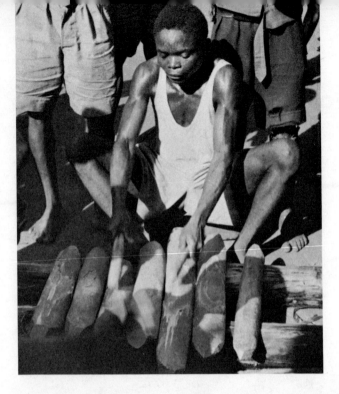

Musical instruments of the Cameroons. Above, a musician plays a tune on a wooden xylophone. Below, instruments of Chung, a secret society of men related to the Fon. The drums make a "voom-voom" sound as the dampened poles are pushed up and down through the leather hides. The double gongs are handbells operated by the leaders of Chung.

hear the story and join in the fun and feasting that were sure to follow. Neba told the tale, and the Fon repeated it in stentorian tones for all to hear. Aboumbi presented his son with a colorful woven cap, a bush-cow drinking horn, and most important of all, the coveted red feather. The leopard skin was given to the king, as befitted his royal status. In fact, no commoner was ever allowed to keep any part of a leopard skin; battles had been fought with other tribes who refused to give up these skins to the Fon. The meat, according to ritual, was cut up and divided between the Fon and the Council of Elders.

After the feast, Ingwa and Kimi, with Neba, sat listening to the old men reminisce about leopard hunting in the old days. Spears were never used, for these animals were so vicious and lightning-quick they could turn against the spear holder and claw him to death before he had a chance to escape. When the tracks of a leopard were sighted, a party was sent out by the Fon to construct a spring trap across the trail. A thick, resilient pole was cut, to which a rope noose, reinforced with wire, was attached near one end, the other end of the pole was embedded upright deep in the ground. The loose end was held down by a forked stick. The open noose, camouflaged, was placed across the trail, so that when the prey stepped on it, the animal was caught and lifted high into the air. When its snarls and roars attracted a hunter, men were sent out by the Fon, sometimes as many as fifty, who finished off the cat with their spears and transported it to the village. Often, other animals were caught in these spring traps; sometimes even a man was snared as he walked along the trail in the late afternoon and failed to see it. But his screams and cries presently brought help.

After Ingwa killed any animal, he always presented a certain portion, usually the head, to his mother's oldest brother. It was this uncle who had given him his first spear, paid his initiation fee into the Chung society, and acted as a second father. It was the Bafut custom for the maternal uncle to train his sister's children as though they were his own. All through his youth, Ingwa and his uncle maintained a close relationship; he always addressed the old man as "father" in a considerate fashion. Soon after Ingwa's initiation, the old fellow became ill, and not long after the presentation of the red feather, he died. His wise companionship was a great loss.

The Burning of Bafut

Although Zintgraff had left the grasslands, other Germans were destined to return. Ivory, kola, palm oil, and other produce were too tempting to the traders, and already the administration was building roads and new stations. Missionaries were close on their heels. The Bali chief, Garega, was cooperating fully with his old friends, and the Germans expected him to assist them in conquering the Bafut.

In 1896, Zintgraff had returned to Bali for a short time. He had been told by the German administrator at Douala that he could not return to the grasslands, because he merely stirred up dissension. But after working as a journalist in South Africa for a few months, he came back to the Cameroons to work for the palm plantations on the coast. From there he journeyed once more to Bali to recruit laborers for the plantations, some few of them Bafut men. And he left some officers and administrators at the little German post Garega had helped build several years before. But he never again visited Bafut. In 1897, on his way to Germany on sick leave, Zintgraff died at sea off the coast of Tenerife. He was thirty-nine years old.

In 1903, Aboumbi and the Council of Elders learned that the number of white men in Bali was increasing. They were gravely concerned over the possibility that the Germans might drag their young men off to the coast, where fever and disease would kill them. Once again a council of war was held, and the military society intensified its drill. By this time, Ingwa and his brothers were accompanying Muma and others on long treks through the grasslands to trade for the Fon. Guns and ammunition, mainly, were the items they sought, for there was a vague uneasiness that the white man would return. But Garega seemed to have cornered the market, and from trip after trip the travelers returned with smaller amounts than the Bafut needed. The smiths were kept busy fashioning knives and spears. The diviners and sorcerers worked feverishly mixing potions to be rubbed on ropes that would be placed across all paths leading into the village, for the malevolent witches were again riding on the winds of spring, bringing evil and disease, possibly even the white man. On each market day the visiting traders were closely watched and astutely questioned for news of activity among the Bali. The Fon regularly cross-examined those traders he felt he could trust; in addition, his own spies were at work. Everyone sensed that it was only a question of time before the Germans, with Garega's assistance, would swoop down on Bafut. They had not long to wait.

The Bande scouts came running into Bafut one market day. They rushed down the path to the royal compound, followed by an immense crowd anxious to hear the news. Aboumbi was caught unawares; he had to be called back from a nearby village. The big signal drum could be heard, thundering through the countryside, summoning the Bukum and all quarterheads to the palace. The messenger brought only bad news: the Germans were marching on Bande. Bali runners had appeared in Bande, announcing that the white man wanted only peace, that he wished only to trade.

The scout paused a moment, and Muma shouted that more likely it was trade for Bande men and then trade for Bafut men. At that, a woman in the back of the crowd began screaming, no, no, and the entire enclosure echoed with shouting and yelling.

The Fon held up his hand and called for silence. The man went on to say that Garega was preparing to send an army to Bande before the next market day to make sure the chief would negotiate with the Germans. He paused for breath and then turned back to the Fon; the Bande chief thought it might be wise to capitulate. Aboumbi shook his head. Never! He had seen too many men dragged off to slavery; he had taken plenty of slaves himself. To him, labor on the coast was merely another form of slavery. He knew it was better to die in battle.

That night the elders, the Bukum, and all the military groups met to plan their strategy. Help must be sent to the Bande people if the grasslands were to be rid of these white men. Before sunup next morning, the messengers started for Bande with nearly five hundred Bafut warriors ready to follow. Chunga and Kimi acted as scouts for the first group of one hundred men, and Ingwa and Ndi were assigned to one of four other groups of one hundred warriors each. These formed into units on the hills just south of the main village of Bafut.

By late afternoon Chunga's unit had passed the three-quarter point. On a little rise where the plateau stretched out for miles around them, they paused and decided to stop. There was a stream nearby and a few compounds where they could get some fruit and spend the night.

In the early morning, cold and stiff, the men rose quickly, filed out of the fiber gates, and silently waited for their orders to move. It was still early, and the fog had not yet left the hills. Chunga was worried by a premonition of something wrong. He had dreamed of a leopard attacking them, a sure sign of disaster. He whispered to Kimi, as they moved on ahead of the others, that Garega was up to no good, and the Germans must be evil and destructive men.

Just then the sun broke over the high escarpment on their left. It was always an awesome sight, this time more magical than ever, with the fog filling the valleys below them and the luminescent sunshine bathing everything in pink and scarlet. Violent and overpowering, the color was reflected in the western sky and then swallowed up in the fog. As the boys looked southward, they thought they saw another, more brilliant sun rising. But the sun doesn't rise in the south. They jogged on, using the loping stride that Bafut men have learned will carry them tirelessly for miles. The fog was lifting rapidly, and the southern sky still glowed with a lurid, red flame.

At that instant two men came over the crown of the hill just ahead. Chunga and Kimi dived into a clump of shrubs, but when they recognized the strangers as Bande men, they came back to the path. The men were rushing to Bafut to warn the Fon that the Germans had, that night, set fire to Bande and were probably, even now, marching north. The four men sprinted back to the Bafut contingent. It was decided to head off the other units, because there was not much aid to be given the Bande people now; Bafut must be alerted.

When the Fon heard the appalling news he immediately ordered the tribe to mobilize for war. The magicians laid across all paths the special magic that would cause the death of any man who stepped over it. The young mothers and their small children, the sick and elderly, all were sent off along the path to the north, into more mountainous terrain, where they would be comparatively safe. The royal wives and the younger enchindas carried what religious objects they could to the security of the hills. Everyone carried as much food as possible.

Two days later the scouts reported that Garega and the Germans were marching up from Bande, moving swiftly and resolutely, as though prepared for battle. The German officer sent a Bali emissary to inform Aboumbi they were coming in peace, that they wanted only to trade with the Bafut. Aboumbi sent the man back with the message that he, the Fon, dictated the terms under which the Bafut would trade. He was not about to open negotiations with his long-time enemies and their allies.

The ensuing battle raged for days. At first, the Bafut hoped the magic spread along the paths would begin to work against the enemy. But also they were pragmatists, and they had prepared for possible war. They relied on their familiarity with their own narrow, winding village paths for some protection. As the Bali warriors approached, there were intermittent sounds of shooting. But there were no people left at that end of the town. The enemy was wasting his ammunition on a few pigs and goats, while hoping to surprise a lone straggler. As they approached the plaza, they were met by a deafening barrage of gunfire from the defending Bafut warriors.

The Fon's bodyguard, a group of fifty or more stalwart fighters, tried to persuade Aboumbi to retreat to a safer place in the hills just north of the town. He refused. All his life he had loved a good fight; now that his people were battling for their lives, he could hardly retreat. On came the Bali. Suddenly Ingwa and Chunga came sprinting around the corner of the market place. They were followed by four Bali men, all trying to get close enough to fire their guns. Kimi saw them. The Fon had sent them to Muma with a message. He fired at the Bali men, killing one. The others ducked behind a wall, while Ingwa and his brother ran into the yard through the back and shot two of them before they could turn around. The last one held his spear aloft, preparing to hurl it at Kimi, who had rushed through the front gate. But Ingwa brought his heavy bush knife down on the man's head and, with one stroke, cut the skull in two. When he looked up, he saw more Bali warriors running past the gate toward the palace. Fearful of what might be happening to the Fon, he yelled to Kimi and Chunga that he would go back through the small door behind the Fon's own house. Kimi went on to find Muma, while Chunga and Ingwa bolted back to the royal compound.

Here they discovered Aboumbi in complete charge of the situation. He was standing in the center of the yard beside a Y-shaped post, one of their most sacred religious objects. Grouped around him was his bodyguard; he was shouting instructions first to one messenger, then to another. He grinned at his sons, then gave more directions for the battle.

When it grew dark, a sultry and disquieting truce took effect. No fires were lit for fear of the enemy's sporadic gunshots. The men ate whatever food they could find and washed it down with palm wine that had not been destroyed. At every turn of the paths, at all the compound gates, sentries stood their watch until dawn broke over the tranquil hills.

The fighting continued. Once, the German officers sent messengers to sue for peace, but Aboumbi arrogantly refused to speak to them and sent them back. After a few days, the Bafut men began to run out of ammunition. This was their ruin, for each time the military societies tried to venture out for hand-to-hand combat, they were driven back by the superior guns of the Bali and the Germans. When he realized this, the Fon reluctantly agreed to save his remaining warriors, and he retreated to the hills. But before they could gather their weapons and their wounded, the Bali set fire to the thatched roofs. The enemy rushed in, killing all they could find; then they burned the remaining huts, including the stately house of the Fon.

A few Germans stayed on near the village for several months. They hoped to establish communication with the Fon of Bafut, but it was a long time coming.

The Bafut people wandered about in the bush for months, subsisting on what food they could forage or beg from their old neighbors, whom they had once subjugated. They were unable to prepare their farms, and all the stored food had been destroyed in the fire. Several times the Fon sent an emissary, sometimes Muma, sometimes Kweyifon, to the officers at the desolated village. But many men had been killed on both sides, and because neither side was willing to accede much, negotiation was difficult.

The people roamed as far north as Menchem Falls, where Ingwa saw, for the first time, the awesome waterfall and pool where the tribal ancestor chiefs were believed to reside. With trepidation the people watched the water pour unendingly through a cleft in the naked, gray volcanic rock sixty feet above them. The roar of the water deafened them all. They stared at the sparkling spray flying out and away from the falls, coming to rest at last in a placid pool some yards downstream; part of the spume was caught against the boulders, rested there momentarily, and then was released to travel on. On both sides of the falls, the hills were studded with lovely trees. Bright little blossoms grew in the crevices next to the water.

Wearily they set up their camp and prepared for the night. At the edge of the pool, the Council of Elders, led by Kweyifon, reverently poured libations of palm wine on the ancestor stones of the last four Fons. Aboumbi guided Ingwa and Chunga to one of the gray stones. In a low voice, which trembled with sorrow, he explained that here rested the souls of their ancestors; here, one day, his soul would repose. He sat for a while, deep in thought, and then he counseled the two young princes to listen to the voices of their ancestors, for they would offer strength and comfort in these times of desolation.

The Germans, meanwhile, built an administrative station and fort high on the Bamenda escarpment, overlooking the little village of Bafreng, one of Bafut's allies. Here and at Bali, the missionaries and traders soon followed the military.

At last, after six months of wandering, Aboumbi called together the Council of Elders. He told them he had decided that, in order to save his people from starvation, he would go alone to Bamenda and give himself up. They pleaded with him in vain; he realized that only a king was high enough ransom for their lives. He was sent to Douala in chains, where he stayed in exile for a year. During that time he was allowed to do a little farming on a nearby plantation; the great Fon of Bafut was suffered to perform a woman's work. The people returned to rebuild their towns and their compounds and repair their farms. In all, three hundred men, as indemnity, were pressed into service for the coastal plantations or put to work building the German fort at Bamenda.

The year passed, during which time Muma and the Council took charge of rebuilding Bafut. Then the men collected a large quantity of ivory, leopard skins, and goats. A delegation took this payment to the German officer at Bamenda and begged him to return the king. The Germans, too, had discovered that orderly government was difficult to achieve without the strong authority of the Fon; so, in a few weeks, negotiations were completed, and Aboumbi, "He Who Rules the World," returned to Bafut.

Murder and Justice

After the Fon's return to Bafut, life flowed more peacefully once again. Once in a while the Germans appeared, to press the king for more men to work at the fort in Bamenda, and laborers were sent to the banana, oil palm, and cocoa plantations on the coast. Rough bush roads began to appear, as did some of the more intangible manifestations of Western civilization: a different language, a strange religion, new laws. The German missionaries at Bali came up to Bafut and established a tiny church in 1904. The Fon was not enthusiastic, but he gave his permission and did not forbid attendance.

A school was already established in Bali, and several Bafut boys were eager to attend. Among them was young Shu, son of the man who specialized in circumcision. He was a bit older than Ingwa, introspective, clever, and intelligent. He realized that it could prove invaluable to have someone in the Bafut tribe able to converse with the Germans. When the mission schoolteachers arrived in Bafut with their announcement, Shu asked his father for permission to go to Bali. The old man consented only on the supposition that it would cost him nothing and that the Fon had no objection. Young Shu thought he would not get any kind of schooling free, but he wisely kept his counsel, merely saying no, the Germans were offering this education free to promising young men. While he was there, however, he would be expected to pay something toward his keep.

The next month four boys from Bafut walked down to the Bali mission. Shu was the only one who stuck it out long enough to return several years later as a full-fledged teacher, but one of the others became very helpful to the Fon, and two were given jobs at the German fort in Bamenda.

In 1912, the mission administrators approached Aboumbi for authority to establish a school in Bafut. They told him Shu would be the teacher. Again the Fon was reluctant. But after Shu pointed out that continued hostility to the Germans would gain them nothing, and that a considerable amount of good could come from an established school, he finally consented. Land in Njinteh quarter was set aside for the small shelter, which was built by the parents as partial payment for their sons' education. Shu was paid a small sum by the German mission, and from time to time a few of the townspeople brought him palm oil and other produce to help defray expenses. The first years, however, were difficult ones for the young man. Often he was on the verge of surrendering to the forces of indifference and veiled hostility.

One day his father came to him with the announcement that the Fon was considering sending one of the princes to Shu's school. In order to help clear up some questions, Shu was to appear at the palace that evening for consultation. The young teacher knew how important this interview could be, for if he had one or two of the Fon's sons in his classes, it would be far easier to persuade other villagers to send their sons.

At dusk the young man went to the palace, carrying a calabash of palm wine and a length of cotton cloth. As he waited in the anteroom for his summons, he talked with a few royal wives and some of the elders. All were brimming over with advice; some thought he was foolish to try influencing old Aboumbi, long noted for his autocratic ways. Several elders, however, thought the Fon's interest in foreign schooling evinced a willingness to adjust to the new order in the grasslands.

When Shu was escorted into the Fon's courtyard, his father was one of those present. The Fon did not appear immediately, but obviously he had given word that the young schoolteacher was to be treated kindly. Everyone greeted him with deference. Two of the wives approached with smiles and filled his cup with palm wine. Finally, two of the younger wives walked out of Aboumbi's private house, followed closely by the chief himself. Immediately, everyone crouched nearly double, clapped three times, then with their hands before their mouths chanted: "Hail to the Fon. Hail to the Fon!"

Aboumbi wore a Cameroons cap on his head. His gown was

an old one, reaching only from his waist to his ankles; it was embroidered with a flamboyant spider design, black on a cloth of pale yellow. This stylized design was used by nearly all the Tikar tribes as an emblem of royalty. Its source was a black, hairy creature about four to six inches long, with a nasty but not fatal bite. Because the spider built its nest beneath the ground, it seemed obvious that it could communicate with the ancestors and spirits who dwelt therein. Throughout nearly all of Central and Western Africa it was thought, and is still considered, to possess supernatural wisdom. It was revered as an intermediary between the divine spirits and the common man. In many areas a death penalty was pronounced on any luckless person, or even an animal, who killed, by accident or design, one of these formidable creatures.

The Fon sat down and placed his feet on the gigantic elephant tusk. With a studied courtesy he greeted the elders and old Shu. Then, with a gentle smile, he slyly remarked that he was surprised to see the young schoolteacher, who usually talked only to the white man. The elders and wives chuckled at this and looked over to see how Shu was taking it. The young man, too, smiled wryly and gazed at the ground; he decided it was the better part of wisdom to let his father do the talking.

Old Shu laughed aloud. He told the Fon his son did speak the white man's language and could do so without an interpreter. It would be all to the good if there were more young men who could do as well. Aboumbi glanced over to see how young Shu liked this. The Fon was a traditionalist, but he knew the advantage of keeping step with certain modern innovations. His year in the German prison had taught him a great deal. Now he was ready to send one of his sons to Shu's school so that someone at court would be familiar with the language, as well as the devious methods of the conquerors. He turned to a fat little wife standing nearby and ordered her to bring in Chunga, Ndi, Neba, and Ingwa.

The teacher knew all four sons. Chunga was nearly as old as he and a valued and trusted friend. Ndi was interested in hunting and medicine; he would, no doubt, make an excellent medicine man. For this reason, Shu felt Ndi would hardly be aroused by "learning the white man's book." Neba and Ingwa were some years younger, but were full of vitality and aware of everything around them.

The Fon had picked four of his finest sons; it flashed upon Shu that among these four was Aboumbi's successor.

Deferentially, Shu began speaking in a low voice through his cupped hands. It was not for him to choose one of the royal sons to be educated in the white man's fashion. All of these young men were so alert, so prudent, so intelligent, and so clever that all would profit from just a year or two of study. The Fon was pleased with the young man's self-effacement; it was not fitting for a Bafut man to blow his own horn. He glanced over at some of the council. They all nodded. The schoolteacher didn't see this, but he had won the first round.

There followed more talk and more wine. Old Shu got to his feet and described how at first he had opposed his son's attendance at the Bali school, partly because it was located in the midst of their old enemies, and in some measure because it was managed by their new ones. But young Shu had prevailed upon him. Peace was the order of the day in the grasslands; if the young generation was to share in molding the future, it must first become more knowledgeable. It must study the white man's ways, keeping that which was advantageous, yet always retaining the best of the old Bafut culture.

Muma arose. He recited at length the fight with the Germans, describing how both Chunga and Ingwa had distinguished themselves. Although they were several years apart in age, he said, Ingwa already possessed much of the wisdom Chunga carried. He suggested the council consider sending both young men to benefit from young Shu's teaching.

It was late. The few wives who remained, the mothers of Ingwa and Chunga among them, were growing restive. They had hoped for a dance that night, but the Fon looked too serious now for such frivolity. Finally, one of the elders suggested that they discuss it with the Fon again in the morning, when no women would be around. Everyone was aware that he also meant to wait until the schoolteacher was absent. And there the matter rested.

Shu went home. Some of the Council of Elders walked with him down the path. The Fon, a few of his wives, the four sons, and the remaining elders drummed and drank and danced for a

while. Then they too drifted off to bed. No one was certain of
the outcome.

About a week later, old Shu appeared at his son's hut. He
carried a small bag of cowrie shells, partial payment for the
schooling the young teacher would give Chunga and Ingwa.
Following Muma's suggestion, the council had urged the Fon to
give both young men the advantage of learning some of the white
man's ways. The teacher was warned not to show any partiality
because they were sons of the Fon. If they evinced an aptness for
learning, there would be additional payment. Delighted, young
Shu told his father when the boys were to come and what they
should bring.

So the schooling began. Each pupil brought food for the
long day. In addition to their lessons, they spent time in calisthen-
ics. Shu had learned the German characteristics of neatness and
organization; these he passed on to his pupils by insisting they
tidy up the school premises.

The students assembled at the little hut just after sunrise
each day. They studied indoors for a while, then took time out to
eat some of the food they brought. After a short session outdoors, they all gathered inside again for intensive work on read-
ing and writing in German. The few books in the Bali language
formed a basis. Arithmetic was an important part of the curricu-
lum, and deportment carried as much weight as all the rest.
When the pupils did not do well, the teacher had them spread-
eagled on the table and gave them a good thrashing with a switch.
The miscreant was held by his fellows, while Shu applied
the rod. Sometimes, because they were the Fon's sons, and therefore expected to perform better than the others, Ingwa and
Chunga received whippings out of all proportion to their misdeeds. The fact that both were nearly as old as the teacher disturbed no one.

Young Shu tried to instill in his students some of the interest
in flowers and trees he had acquired from the Germans. Birds and
animals were well known to all the Bafut, for they came from
generations of hunters. But the esthetic qualities of nature did not
come easily to them. Shu was an extremely articulate teacher, and
to most of his students he proved a vital and sound example. He
showed them how to mark the schoolyard paths with stones,

how to plant shrubs and flowers, how to keep the hut itself clean and neat. In the tropical lushness, brilliant hibiscus and dappled croton gave a gardenlike effect to the schoolyard.

Ingwa enjoyed this, for he had always appreciated, in a small way, the beauty of his mountain home. Now he learned to see the birds not as a hunter but as an observer. The sunbirds, with their sparkling turquoise wings, were jewel-like even in leafy shade. They skimmed rapidly over the bushes, lighting ever so gently at each flower, where, with twittering, musical calls they searched for nectar. The busy, frantic weaverbirds anxiously stripped the palm fronds in their quest for nesting materials. Ingwa watched as tremendous flocks worked on a single tree. Screeching and haranguing in their harsh, rasping voices, they built long, hanging nests. Soon the tree was completely decorated by these nests, which entirely replaced the elegant green plumage of the palm branches. He watched the colorful geckos, those small, harmless lizards that were present at every turn of the path and in every hut, where their presence was considered good luck. They pranced and nodded like jesters trying to please the king. Down near the stream, Ingwa liked to see the funny little toads and frogs that scurried from behind the fallen logs and from under the stones. Some had huge popeyes, and some had tiny warts; others wore red dots along their backs; still others had beautiful creamy undersides.

Once, on their way to school, he and Chunga noticed a big, furry black spider scrambling off the path. They watched it scuttle off to its burrow a few inches away. This was the sacred spider used to determine the future. Bafut boys were always curious about this, and when Chunga suggested they consult the spider, Ingwa agreed. No special diviner was necessary. With a stick, the two drew lines radiating from the hole. At the end of each line they placed a twig. While they waited for the spider to reappear, they decided upon which path the creature must travel in order to answer their questions. Ingwa wondered which of them would succeed their father. Chunga refused to tell what his question was. When the spider finally came out, the youths had been whispering together; each forgot to keep track of his particular line. The spider ran over the twigs and out of sight, while the tardy pupils boisterously pushed each other off the path.

When they reached school, they were late again, and Shu obliged them with another beating.

For a little over a year, Ingwa attended school with Chunga. Then, abruptly, Aboumbi demanded the presence of them both at court. Ingwa was now living out in the village with one of his mother's brothers, for he had passed the age when he could stay in the royal compound. Early each morning he went to the palace. Although he was not an enchinda, he helped them in their duties, and in this way he learned much of the tribal routine. He ate his meals in his mother's hut, with two of his younger brothers. This pleased him, for he had little time these days to visit with his family. In addition, the Fon ordered Ingwa to accompany him on his rounds of the compound and the village. These were not always daily visits, but at least weekly, unless judicial or martial duties kept him from it, Aboumbi surprised some area of the village with a tour of inspection.

As they sauntered down the path, followed by one or two enchindas and an older palace retainer, the Fon often gave long discourses on his duties as keeper and protector of the Bafut tribe. Not only was he the divine chief, religious leader, and nominal father of the tribe, but he was also responsible for its moral well-being and physical fortunes. The chief investigated the kitchen gardens, the fences surrounding each enclosure, and the animals along the way. He inspected the paths and roads leading from one part of the village to another. He scrutinized the ditches that drained off the torrents of rain water. He listened constantly for signs of squabbling, kept an alert ear and eye for behavior that might merit a reward; he scolded a naughty child here and smiled on a good deed there. In short, although he had spies and henchmen in every quarter to do these things for him, the sudden and unexpected appearance of the king was always an excellent way to keep the people on their toes.

This morning, when they returned to the palace, they saw more than the usual number of men crowding around the gates. One of the messengers hurried up to Aboumbi and, crouching low in the Bafut manner, told him a murder had been committed the night before. Murder in Bafut was most unusual. Disconcerted, the Fon immediately ordered all persons connected with it to report to his palace that afternoon. He also sent for the Bukum, in case any judicial questions might arise.

Around four o'clock, after the heat of the day, all important men of the tribe were packed into the Fon's private enclosure. When Aboumbi appeared on the steps of his house, he was dressed in an impressive robe of gorgeous purple, heavily encrusted with Cameroons symbols embroidered in gold. He wore the Cameroons cap on his head, his feet were encased in intricately beaded leather boots, and he carried a simple wooden staff. He gazed arrogantly down at the throng of waiting men. Then slowly he descended the basalt steps to his carved stool under the fig tree. He was angry, and a ripple of fear swept through the crowd. Aboumbi knew that any rumors of murder might soon reach the Germans, and he was determined not to have any interference from them on the Bafut way of dealing with the slayer. He still bore traumatic scars of his year at Douala.

As he sat down, he asked in a loud, haughty voice who had committed this murder. A cowering man was torn bodily from the crowd and pushed to the ground before the king. He was about thirty, chocolate-colored rather than the deep, sooty black of most of the Bafut people. His eyes were furtive, and on one cheek he bore a deep scar from a knife wound sustained in a drunken brawl. The Fon recognized Nbangi, the son of a man who had married a female slave from Adamawa in the north; she had been given by the Fon in exchange for a great favor. The son was free, however, and had never born the stigma of slavery. The women and children obtained as war captives were generally retained as slaves, the boys either becoming enchindas or being adopted into other families. They were not looked upon as slaves thereafter. The girls and women were invariably distributed in marriage by the Fon. If anyone called them slaves subsequently, the husband had a good case for libel, and the insult was generally avenged in a violent manner.

The Fon shouted for someone to tell the story. He refused to have a live murderer in Bafut beyond another market day. One of the quarterheads, a member of the Bukum, stepped forward and proceeded to relate the events as told him by the wives and sons of the murdered man. It was a long story, embellished with asides into the personal histories of each family.

Nbangi, although he was a free man, had always resented the fact that his mother was a slave. This made him quarrelsome and somewhat of a bully. His father had not been able to afford more than two wives, and their constant bickering seemed to have rubbed off on Nbangi. He was not liked in his own quarter, and he worked overtime trying to extort palm wine from his relatives without giving any in return. On the other hand, Fawnkum, his neighbor, was well regarded among his fellow men; he had three wives, who had presented him with several children and who were obviously fond of each other. They were thrifty, their farms were models of good agriculture, their children were hard working and well behaved.

Nbangi had inherited the compound of his father several years before. He had had difficulty taking care of it, partly because he had but one wife, whom he beat so mercilessly that she spent most of her time out on her farm. Once he had had another wife, but she ran back to her family when she realized she had been married nearly two years without becoming pregnant. In Bafut, as indeed throughout much of West Africa, a woman's dearest wish, and reason for being, is to have a child; barrenness is a catastrophe. Yet, difficult though it is for a childless woman to face the community, for a man it is worse; he often becomes a laughing stock in the market place and the palm-wine huts. "You are not fit to drink with us," the men taunt him. "You cannot produce children!" Nbangi's first wife had borne a child, but only one, and there were rumors that it was not Nbangi's.

Apparently Fawnkum's good fortune so preyed on Nbangi's mind that he resolved to do something about it. One evening he invited Fawnkum to drink palm wine with him. Never one to think ill of his neighbor, Fawnkum accepted the invitation, surmising that Nbangi had finally decided to settle for a peaceful coexistence. They drank far into the night.

As Nbangi drank more wine, he began to find fault with his neighbor far beyond any he had mentioned before. Fawnkum didn't like the turn of events, and having said so, he decided to leave—he realized that a drunken Nbangi would be dangerous. But he had drunk too much wine himself. Apparently, as he tried to leave the hut, he stumbled—whereupon Nbangi, in a rage, began to beat him with his fists. As poor Fawnkum tried to rise to

defend himself, his oldest wife entered the hut. She had hea
their voices in her own compound, and she thought she cou
persuade her husband to come home with her. Just as she push
aside the fiber door, she saw Nbangi reach for the ancestor sto
which was always kept between the fireplace and door. I
brought it crashing down on Fawnkum's skull. The w
screamed hysterically, bringing her co-wives, the neighbors, a
Nbangi's wife rushing to the scene. But it was too late. Fawnku
was dead, the victim of a murder cunningly planned. Killing w
the ancestor stone was too much. No one ever touched that sto
except to pour libations upon it in reverence to one's ancesto

It was probably his malicious use of the ancestor sto
coupled with his past history of being an undesirable member
the community, that sealed Nbangi's fate. He might have gott
off with a severe beating, the punishment usually meted out o
charge of killing a man in a drunken brawl. But there were t
many testimonials about his ill will toward Fawnkum, his ob
ous jealousy of the other's better fortune. Nbangi and his broth
pleaded in vain for his life. The Bukum had no sympathy
such a man. They nodded in agreement when the Fon p
nounced sentence. Nbangi was to be tied between two trees
the market place until next market day. Then, before the ent
assembly, the king himself would inflict a small wound on
prisoner's shoulder with his cutlass. Two of the Bukum wou
finish the killing. Finally, the crowd would have the opportun
of tearing him to pieces. The remains were to be thrown i
the river, far below the village.

When he heard the verdict, the terrified Nbangi tore hims
from the hands of his guards and threw himself at the feet of
king. Placing both hands on Aboumbi's feet, he cried:

"I didn't mean it. I killed him accidentally! If I do not spe
the truth, may your feet cause my stomach to swell until I di
It was an old Bafut oath, protesting one's innocence, but the
roarious crowd refused to listen. Ingwa yelled his approval;
knew it was only just.

Nbangi was dragged out to the market place immediate
where his brother and his brother's wife brought him little bits
food in the dead of night. They were too ashamed to show the
selves during the day. Nbangi's remaining wife had taken I

child back to her family as soon as the verdict was pronounced.

Three days later the sentence was carried out before a throng of nearly five thousand people, most of whom had never seen a murderer. It was a wild and dreadful market day. Very little trading took place; everyone stood around taunting the victim, waiting for the Fon to appear. After he and the Bukum had performed their ritual killing, the tumultuous crowd rushed in with the eagerness of warriors answering the call to battle. Even the women and children pushed forward to fling stones and insults at the bloody, mangled corpse. When the men returned from the river, the market place was being cleaned up. No one ventured near it for a day or two.

A month or two later there was more excitement in the market. Ingwa, with his friend Kimi, watched Kweyifon bring in a man from an outlying village, a man accused of stealing a goat from his neighbor. Thieves were rare in Bafut, and usually a mere warning was enough for the first offense. The second misdemeanor was punished by imprisonment in public stocks until restitution had been made. Because this was the man's second offense, Kweyifon was determined to try a different maneuver.

Four sticks were placed in the ground, with the miscreant cowering in the center. These were magical sticks that placed so strong a spell upon the thief that he dared not move. All day, in the hot sun, the thief remained within the square, the object of ridicule and derision. Finally, in the late afternoon, his wife arrived, leading the stolen animal by a tether. Kimi and Ingwa cheered with the other onlookers. They all listened to Kweyifon deliver a strong discourse on the evils of thieving. As he released the prisoner from his spell, Kweyifon warned that next time he would either be killed in the market place or sold into slavery in Adamawa.

Other serious misdeeds were similarly dealt with, the discipline being varied to fit the crime. The assault of one man upon another was punished, at times, by imprisonment in the public stocks until the victim's wounds healed and a goat was paid as compensation. However, in a warlike tribe like the Bafut, it was possible for the victim to settle the matter in his own way and still be within his rights. With a group of his friends, he could obtain retribution in a small but honorable fracas with the followers of his assailant. The king did not interfere as long as the quarrel was settled without serious injury.

Witchcraft, however, was another matter. Ingwa vividly remembered the time an old neighbor of his uncle's had consulted a male witch in another village. The neighbor, who wanted a long-time enemy killed, had not gone to the diviner, who was a power for good, but to one reputed to be a witch. Ingwa's uncle described how the witch prepared a bowl of water with a magic powder in it. As the client pronounced the name of the man he wanted dispatched, the image of the luckless victim appeared in the water. With a sharp three-inch iron needle, the witch pierced the water. By sympathetic magic, the enemy died—not immediately, but a few months later after a violent fever.

The victim's sons pointed their fingers at the old man and forced him to disclose whom he had consulted. When they caught the witch, they dragged him into Kweyifon's hut in the royal compound. He was forced to drink a cup of poison sassywood and then prodded into walking up a small hill. If he had vomited and recovered, he would have been regarded as innocent and thereby acquitted; but the old fellow died, thus proving his guilt. His client, the old man who caused all the trouble, paid a heavy fine.

Sometimes, such minor offenses as tapping a palm tree that belonged to someone else were resolved by forcing the sassywood poison down the throat of a fowl which belonged to the offender. If the fowl died, the guilt was proved; if it lived, the misdoer was acquitted. All these punishments were carried out by the secret society under the orders of Kweyifon, but they all carried the tacit approval of the king.

Exile

As long as the grassland tribes kept their skirmishings to a minimum, and the traders' wealth in ivory and other produce continued down the winding footpaths to the coast, the German administrators preferred not to interfere with tribal life. Ingwa continued the routine life of a young Bafut man. He drummed and danced as well as the best of them. His reputation as a hunter was growing. He had several stands of palm trees, which he tended when his duties at court were not too pressing; otherwise, he asked his younger brother, Boombi, to care for them, and Boombi was given a share of the proceeds. Ingwa built himself a hut in his uncle's compound and began thinking about a wife. Many village girls were ready to leap at the chance of marrying one of the Fon's sons. But the spirited Ingwa relished a life without ties and kept postponing the idea of marriage. In fact, he hadn't yet found a girl he thought worthy of the large bride price he would be expected to pay her father.

Premarital sexual relations were far from uncommon in old Bafut society, but among royalty it was frowned upon. Bafut girls were often given in marriage as early as six or seven years, although the marriage was not consummated until after they reached puberty. A great many town girls were not married until nearly sixteen or seventeen. In contrast, the excessive bride price sometimes asked by the father made it difficult for a young man to claim his bride much before he was twenty-three or twenty-four years old.

One of the wives of Ingwa's uncle, a charming girl named Bisi, had recently given birth to twins, a boy and a girl. Naturally, everyone expected that, according to tradition, when the children reached eight or nine years, the girl would be pledged to

the Fon to become one of his wives, and the boy would be sent
the royal compound for training as an enchinda. This was
honor not to be taken lightly in Bafut. No one could remembe
time when it was not so; twins were the "gifts of the gods" a
as such, were well treated and highly regarded. They w
"magic" people, despite the extra burden it meant for the moth
Therefore, everyone rejoiced when twins were born.

From far down the path leading to his uncle's compoui
Ingwa heard an unearthly rumpus there. Women returning fr
their farms were soon as distraught as those who had stay
home. In addition to four wives and their children, Ingwa's un
was caring for his mother, two young unmarried sisters, and
old uncle, so there were plenty of people to keep up
pandemonium.

Apparently Bisi had taken it into her foolish head not
present her twins to the Fon, even though the separation wo
not occur for several years. Her husband was roaring angrily
her. She knew the twins would be well received and gain prest
and security. As an enchinda, the boy would have an opportun
of becoming a member of the Bukum, perhaps travel through
entire grasslands with the Fon. If he did his work well, he wo
be richly rewarded with guns, land, possibly a wife. The
could give birth to a future Fon. What more could any mot
want?

Poor Bisi only moaned louder and louder, pressing her t
babies to her breast. She was a pretty girl, perhaps seventeen
eighteen, tall and neatly plump. She had a broad, yet small n
smooth skin the color of midnight, and a playful twinkle in
eyes. Her husband always treated her kindly. On their marri
he had given her land close to the village; this enabled her to
turn from her farm quickly, so she was usually in the compo
to accommodate him when he desired her. There had never b
difficulty before. In spite of a small jealousy on the part of
first wife, all the women genuinely liked each other. One of t
now put her arm around Bisi, crying with her, trying to com
her.

Through her tears Bisi moaned that her daughter would
nothing but a drudge for the other women, the boy just a slav
the Fon. He would be deprived of a chance to go to school in

village. What if he did join the Bukum? She wanted him to go to school, *ai-i-ee-ee!* And her screams pierced the compound fences and bounced back to the house walls, shrilly and sharply. Her unfortunate husband shook his head, frowning. So that was it! That was what came of allowing his wife to attend the new mission church. She wanted her children to attend their school, too.

Bisi nodded her head and rocked her shapely body from side to side. Her lovely face was swollen now from crying. The two little babies began adding their tiny screams to the din. The number-one wife sided with their husband, but the others agreed with Bisi that it was time to stop giving all the twins to the Fon. There were plenty of people in the palace entourage to do the work; besides they could get a higher bride price for the girl twin than the Fon was apt to return in the form of gifts. Sometimes, indeed, if the family was not well off, the chief returned the girl for this economic reason. Apparently, the women were determined to stick together.

Now a crying woman the world over is a terror to her husband, and the men of Bafut are no exception. Ingwa's uncle had listened to the bedlam all afternoon, and it wearied him. Besides, he knew there was nothing he could do about changing the custom; when the twins reached the proper age, one would be pledged to the Fon for a wife and the other would enter royal service. But in the meantime, there must be peace in his compound. He begged Bisi to stop her nonsense. Finally he promised she could send the boy to school before he became an enchinda, but he would not pay for it.

Fuming, he turned to his nephew, who stood watching the uproar. No one was aware that this might be the first crack in what eventually would be the breakdown of the enchinda system; that was in the future. Ingwa was more interested in the manner in which Bisi, with a few tears, could bend her husband to her own will. She was smiling now, a small, secret smile. As she nuzzled each one of the babies, she peered up at her husband and thanked him prettily. She knew he would keep his promise, because it was given before witnesses. She wished only that, because she couldn't share his bed for another year and a half, she could buy one of those new European cloths in the market.

Her husband, with Ingwa, had already started toward his

own hut, so glad was he to have quieted her, but he stopped and grinned at her artfulness. All Bafut men, royalty and commoners alike, preferred their wives to dress in their traditional bead gir-dles or short skirts made of woven fiber. These tastes seemed to be based purely on economics. After all, it cost a lot of money to buy cloth for many wives and daughters. A few village women had begun to wear a cotton cloth pulled tight across their breasts, with their babies fastened snugly and securely on their backs, rather than in the little antelope sling. If he refused the cloth, Ingwa's uncle knew Bisi would start all over again. He laughed and promised her cloth money on next market day.

As the compound quieted down and the wives began pound-ing their cocoyams for the evening meal, they chattered in low voices about Bisi's rebellion. They didn't envy her the cloth, for they knew that, by the same kind of performance, each could ex-tort some special favor. But they were overwhelmed at her shrewdness in being able to extract a promise of white man's schooling for her son. What if it was several years hence? In time the whole village would know, and the promise would have to be kept. A few of the women frowned on the idea, but the younger ones agreed that a little European education, in addition to the traditional Bafut training, was not a bad thing.

It was 1915. As Ingwa hurried to the royal compound, in answer to an urgent message from his father, he recognized some visitors as men from Laikom. It was here, where the Kom tribe lived, about twenty-five miles over the mountains, that the Bafut tribe had stopped for a while, during their long journey three hundred years before. Kom was an important kingdom, perhaps not as powerful as Bafut, although no Kom man would ever let it be said in his presence. The two tribes traded together and ex-changed slaves, beads, and the famous Kom cloth. Bafut admitted the superiority of Kom in the field of wood carving, for in these mountains lived the most skillful craftsmen.

Aboumbi explained that several Bukum from Laikom brought the sad news that one of their important elders had died. The first "die-cry," or funeral, would be held in four days. Ingwa was to represent the Fon of Bafut.

In the tropics the dead are buried immediately, and among

Tikar tribes, the die-cry is held about a week later. This affords friends and relatives time to collect food, gifts, and gunpowder to shoot, thus providing an honorable requiem for the departed spirit. About a year later, a second funeral is held to assure a fitting repose for the dead ancestor and to guarantee health and good luck to the remaining relatives. If the second die-cry is not held, there is a possibility of sickness in the family, hard luck, barrenness, or even death, all caused by the ill-tempered ancestor who may have been angered by the lack of reverence.

Ingwa knew that being chosen to act as the personal representative of the king was a great honor. Among the Fon's half a hundred sons there was always considerable wrangling and sparring. The Tikar tradition of secretly designating the chief's successor worked a certain hardship on those sons who were eager for wealth, power, and prestige. Each man knew his chances of succeeding to the royal throne were minimized by the mere existence of all his brothers. The rivalry often took such sinister forms as physical violence, even assassination; more than one son of the king had met an "accidental" death, eaten poison stew, or died from an evil sorcerer's spell. So, in order to confuse them all and protect the chosen one (whose identity was known only to the Fon and two senior Bukum), it became the custom to send several sons into protective exile for a period of years. Ostensibly, they acted as emissaries for their father; in reality they were removed from their bloodthirsty brothers. Occasions like the Kom funeral masked this practice of protective custody.

Nor could any of the sons be warned of their danger, for any hint of the successor's identity could prove fatal. Too many unscrupulous brothers carried on intrigues, bribing anyone they could corrupt within the palace. This removal of a son from Bafut also gave the king an opportunity to study the reports returned by his associate chiefs.

Ingwa knew full well that he could be going into such exile. But on the other hand, there was the possibility that on this journey he was exactly what he appeared to be: a diplomatic delegate at a funeral. He returned his brothers' malevolent looks with a cheerful grin.

Before he left the compound, Ingwa visited his mother. Ashoh gave him food for the journey and a calabash of palm

wine. For such a burden of gifts as the occasion demanded, the
was a long line of marchers. Each man carried a heavy load. Sor
also led live goats; a few, fat-tailed sheep. In the morning, t
secret societies would follow with drums and more gifts, partic
larly gunpowder.

The sun had arisen and had already begun to touch the we
ern hills with morning gold and bronze as they wound their w
out of the village toward the northeast. The air was placid. T
radiant sunbirds were flashing among the white and yellow bl
soms. High above the Fon's tall house came the mourning dov
melancholy calls. The weaverbirds stirred restlessly in one
their denuded palm trees.

The long line of men strode silently toward the mountai
They were all sturdy hunters, accustomed to walking great d
tances with heavy loads on their heads. Their bare feet made o
faint sounds on the paths. Each man carried a staff with which
balanced himself when it was necessary. Up the mountains a
down into the valleys along the streams they filed, stopping o
in the heat of the day to rest and eat. News of the reason
their journey traveled before them, and along the way, peo
came out to offer cool water, fruits, and tart, refreshing pa
wine. The Laikom men formed another line behind them, car
ing more gifts from the Fon of Bafut to the Fon of Kom and
the bereaved family.

The road to Kom wound over several mountain ranges,
rocky and wild and extremely beautiful even in the dry season
was just before the burning of the grass, when great fires wo
light the sky at night as the hillsides were readied for the n
planting season. This burning also drove the game down into
valleys, so that it served the twofold purpose of clearing the fie
and simplifying the hunters' tasks. It is thought that just a f
hundred years ago these mountains were covered with verd
but that, over the generations, this firing had turned the area i
what it is today, the grasslands. Huge granite rocks, pushed to
surface by ancient volcanic action, burst through the hills
stood like gigantic human figures above the red earth. The gi
was yellow and sere, with just a few hardy flowers beginning
bloom, thirsty for the spring rains. Here and there fig tr
pines, bombax, and acacia stood out against the light-blue s

Down along the streams in the valleys, raffia palms and a few kola trees stretched like a dark shroud. The harmattan, the hot, dry wind from the Sahara in the north, was at its climax. The horizon appeared cloudy, almost the color of their milky-looking palm wine.

When the men halted for the night, they lodged in one of the numerous villages along the way. In the hut set aside for the warriors' secret societies, a hut taboo to women, they could sit smoking and drinking, retelling the tales of the bravery of the man whose funeral ceremonies they would soon attend. Outside in the night, the sibilant rustling of the trees, the wind coming down from the mountains, the creakings and murmurings of some beast or night bird lent a mysterious air.

Being in an alien village gave Ingwa a strange sense of isolation as he listened to his comrades. He could distinguish, a few yards away, the high, lilting voices of women as they teased and mocked each other. Once in a while there was the deep, soothing voice of a man talking quietly to a younger son. There was a mother's low utterance as she whispered a lullaby to her baby and then the child's convulsive cry before it slipped into sleep. One of the men began to slap a drum softly with his hand. As the pulsating rhythm soothed him to sleep, Ingwa reflected that never had he felt so alive, so content.

At the end of the second day, the men approached Laikom. Long ago, the chief of Kom had carved a hilltop kingdom from giant rocks on a prominence over half a mile above the surrounding plateau. Here he was safe from marauding invaders. Rock had been used in devious ways to shape and construct the compound. The military house was supported by intricately carved wooden pillars. The door frame of each mud hut was cunningly incised with figures depicting the spider, python, leopard, and other Tikar symbols. Red camwood had been rubbed on certain designs, with some parts colored with lime and plant ash, others burnished with the black of charred wood. All of it gave the village a vigorous and dramatic appearance. As a backdrop, in every direction, were the purple hills, the dark trees flowing along the valleys, or a waterfall or two glistening like silver threads on dusky velvet.

In the enormous compound, preparations were already under

way for the funeral celebration of the dead man; he had been a son of the old Fon of Kom, an important quarterhead and an influential man in the Chung society. Food and drink were carried in by the women. Colorful lengths of cotton cloth, beads, and ivory were piled near a doorway. Nearly every man there had a gun, for now firearms were found everywhere since their introduction a couple of generations before.

The party from Bafut went directly to the military house and rested until the sun had set. Then, arrayed in fresh clothing, they carried their gifts to the Fon, who received them graciously. Ingwa was presented with two enchindas, fine Jukun cloth, and a large ivory tusk that had not been carved. It would be cut when Ingwa decided on the emblems he thought suitable for his father. Other presents might be added after the Fon surveyed the Bafut offerings, but this was an excellent beginning.

After the evening meal of fruit, roasted goat, cocoyams, and palm wine, the men sat talking of their dead friend. One of the Bafut societies had not brought their musical instruments with them, the xylophone with wooden slats, so arrangements were made to use a local one. The Kom men were eager to be of assistance, for they knew that in traveling such a distance, the men of Bafut had paid them a great tribute. Exhausted, yet exhilarated, the men retired for the night.

The next day, the day of mourning, would also be a day of honor to the dead man, his family, the chief, and the tribe. Like much of West Africa, the people of Kom and Bafut considered "life" the greatest good, and this man had lived a long, fruitful, and honorable one. Therefore, the coming ceremony would not be a sad occasion, but one of rejoicing that he was able to live out his time. Much deference would be given his memory so that his descendants, in the years to come, would be blessed with good luck and prosperity.

The next morning, almost an hour before sunrise, people began to pour into the dead man's compound. The secret societies to which he belonged gathered in their ritual costumes. Ingwa prepared to dance with the local Chung society, for the dead man had been an important member of that group.

In Laikom, the head of Chung was an officious old man, but he knew how to organize. First, he checked costumes to be sure each man was properly dressed. Then, the Father of the Chung, as he was called, donned his fiber hood and feathered cloak; atop his head he wore a heavy, beautifully carved wooden mask whose features seemed frozen in a smiling grimace. Grasping the double handbell and its padded beater, he began singing the song that announced the Chung society was ready to dance. In addition to the gongs, Chung had friction drums, the "Body of Chung." Each consisted of a log section about a foot and a half in diameter and a foot high; the top was covered with leather hide, and through this was thrust a pole about an inch in diameter. This pole was dampened slightly with water. As the drummer pushed it up and down, there came forth from the vibrating drumhead a great *voom-voom* sound. When Ingwa heard it he chuckled; at home, the Bafut would say of it, "Chung was passing gas."

As they gathered in the compound, another society lined up behind them, preparing to dance. Only one man wore a mask and cloak, and the others prepared to move about through the compound searching for the spirit of the deceased, which, of course, was never found.

Still another secret society came up with drums and xylophones. Some of these men had spectacular headdresses of feathers three feet long. Chicken feathers had been dyed and cleverly fastened together to form a colorful crimson spray splashing out from the dancers' heads. As they moved, the feathers swayed back and forth across the sea of dancers like sunlit foam on a darkened ocean. There were others in fiber hoods, anklets of kola kernels jangling as they moved. Some had on their heads heavy carved wooden masks that jumped slightly with the movements of the dancers' bodies. All of these men were sons of the chief, but only certain ones were elected to join this particular, proud society.

The women of the village were gathering, too, bringing green and yellow plantains, red peppers, baskets filled with white, pounded cocoyams, gourds of dark-brown palm oil for the stews. Calabashes of palm wine were brought in. The sons of the deceased had several goats ready for slaughter. All the mourners showed their respect for the dead by wearing ashes smeared over parts of their bodies. The women from the village immediately joined the bereaved widows and daughters and began wailing and

lamenting; the men helped prepare the musical instruments,
the younger boys tumbled and scurried back and forth like li
cane rats.

Suddenly there was a hush. From out beyond the yard ca
a weird tooting on an ivory drone trumpet. It seemed to float
a banshee's eerie call over the thatched roofs. Two long-dra
out notes were sounded as the men came prancing into the c
pound yard. A little baby, dawdling near the food pile, wa
startled that he fell into a heap of bananas as he struggled to
out of their path. The crowd whooped with laughter while
mother scolded him for being an obstacle to important n
Then she hugged him tightly as he hid his face in her gene
breasts.

The men with guns began to shoot, honoring the dece
by firing large quantities of gunpowder. Because the ammuni
was expensive, only the richest could afford it, but these pros
ous men of the village sought prestige by displaying their we
in this way. For most men it took months to acquire enough
munition to make any kind of a showing, and often an exhibi
of this kind would have to be delayed for a year until the far
held the second funeral. As the son of a Fon, Ingwa had plent
powder to shoot.

All day the wailing, dancing, and shooting, and the gyrat
and songs continued. As one society exhausted itself with its sh
manship, another took its place. A group of jesters dressed in
tumes of dried plantain leaves and with fantastic painted des
on their faces added comic relief to the somber proceedings:
crawled along the ground like crabs; they leaped high in th
like antelopes; they scampered through the crowd like monk
They begged for scraps of food, or small beads or shells.
and then they coughed loudly, a signal of disdain, meaning, "
despise death! When we die, it will be as nothing!" This wa
in fun, of course, and everyone knew it.

Finally, when it seemed the throng must be comple
drained of energy, the men announced that the feast was re
The omnipresent palm wine had been flowing freely for s
time. Most of the dancers had already slipped away to get ot
their costumes. Many of the mourners had gone to the ne
stream to wash off their ashes. Now they squatted around

yard and waited for the women to serve the food. In low tones they praised the dead man, remarking on what a fine die-cry he had been given. Now the sons could carry themselves proudly, because their father's spirit would not roam the world but would protect them from evil spirits, for he had been shown supreme honor and respect.

Following the funeral ceremony, the men of Bafut stayed in Kom for over a week, resting, visiting friends, and preparing for the home journey. Unknown to Ingwa, the senior Bukum who accompanied him held a long conversation with the Kom chief. Aboumbi had arranged for Ingwa to remain in Kom for a year or more. It had been discovered that some of Ingwa's brothers were planning to do him mischief. In order to mislead them, the Fon had sent Chunga to Bande, Ndi to Babanki, and several others to villages even farther away.

When Ingwa learned that he was to reside in Kom for at least a year, perhaps more, he felt suddenly remote and foreign in this village, where he had known such a happy week. Instantly he understood the implication of his detention. In his private thoughts he vowed that if chosen, eventually, to succeed his father, he would prove worthy of the honor. But to the Bukum he nodded in an unruffled way and merely asked where he was to stay for the next year. Once more the Bukum were impressed with his composure. Another mark went down in his favor.

Life in Kom was similar to life in Bafut. The spring hunt to bring in meat for the chief was held somewhat earlier, but it was a successful one, and with his prowess, Ingwa nearly overshadowed the men of Kom. He tried his hand at wood carving, trying to compete with the finest carvers in the grasslands. However, his thumbs kept intruding, so he gave it up.

With the young girls of Kom he was more successful. Although he was not particularly anxious to be married, several overtures were made by the uncles of some of the loveliest maidens in the village. Ingwa was flattered. Despite his assets as the son of a paramount chief and his frank, open manner, he had not slept with any girl up to this time. The temptation to do so was hard to resist at times, for the girls were lovely flirts. His Kom friends teased him unmercifully. Some suggested he lacked virility, insinuating that he'd make a poor Fon, indeed, if he couldn't impregnate a woman. Crude and humorous little songs were composed during their dances; but always he bore their gibes with good nature, shouting back with glee some ribald jest that set them all laughing with him, not at him.

During his year in Kom, he witnessed a women's uprising that was unique in the grasslands and seen only rarely during one's lifetime. It made so deep an impression on Ingwa that he resolved, should he become Fon, never to allow such a thing to happen in Bafut.

Anlu, as it was called, was a potent force for good, in the old days. It was a Tikar disciplinary technique by which the women could exert an extreme form of social pressure. By taking matters into their own hands they punished someone (usually a man) who had broken certain moral rules. The transgressions included beating or insulting a parent, flogging a pregnant woman, acting incestuously, impregnating a nursing mother within two years after the birth of her child, or abusing old women. The person assaulted could sound a sort of war cry by beating her lips with her fingers and uttering a high-pitched scream.

Fen, a young Kom woman, six months pregnant, was returning home one afternoon from her farm. As she approached her hut, she passed a group of young men who had spent the day drinking. All of them were in poor shape, but Beluh, well known as the village bully, went out of his way to push her against the wall because she didn't move fast enough. The men laughed hilariously at this new game. Poor Fen tried to slip past them before they struck her again, but her heavy body made her clumsy, and they jeered her unmercifully. Suddenly, Beluh, remembering that she had once rebuffed his advances, began to beat her in earnest. He flailed her with his fists, then searched the ground for a stick, while the others, in their stupor, stood by and watched him.

A couple of women on the other side of the wall heard Fen's screams and peered around the gate. They saw the fracas and immediately let out a war cry, which summoned other women to their aid. With heavy sticks and stones they all rushed to the rescue. Fen had lost consciousness and had fallen in a heap to the ground. They carried her tenderly to her compound. That night she aborted. When the women in her quarter heard about the miscarriage, they decided to invoke Anlu.

Beluh's punishment was the subject of lengthy discussion. Because Fen had lost the child, it was an extremely serious offense. The Anlu leader, a dynamic little person with squinty eyes and fancy braids that stood out around her head like tiny snakes, decided that Beluh should apologize to Fen and, in addition, pay an indemnity of six goats, ten fowl, and two calabashes of palm oil. The payment was higher than it would have been had the victim not lost her unborn child. But children were wealth in Kom, so the restitution was higher than the average.

Beluh, however, chose to ignore the Anlu summons, for he considered the affair a paltry one. This made the women so furious that they hastened in a body to the Kweyifon and told him what they were planning to do. He was a wise old man. Carefully he judged their complaints. He agreed that it was a terrible deed and that Beluh must be made to pay for the loss of the child. This kind of thing could not be tolerated in Kom. He stepped into his house and brought out a small drum, which he handed to the Anlu leader, thus giving the women his official sanction. With his drum, they could call the women to Anlu and cleanse the village of its shame.

That night, the women of Fen's quarter and from several quarters nearby, about two hundred in all, met with the leader to plan their attack. In six days they were to meet again, wearing articles of men's clothing, with vines around their shoulders, and carrying a type of wild fruit known as "garden eggs." These were prickly little ovals, light-green in color, with a slightly rancid odor when broken open.

On the day of the assault, as dawn broke, two hundred avenging women advanced on Beluh's compound. He heard them coming and rushed out the back gate. The women, screaming their war cry, trampled his yard, overturning his water gourds and shedding their vines and garden eggs. A few vines were hung over the threshold as a sign that Anlu had been there. His wife decided to join Anlu, and she threw a few tendrils over her shoulders. From Beluh's compound the mob marched on to the neighboring houses, warning the occupants to leave him strictly alone, or Anlu would visit them.

The next week, the Anlu women mobilized at the edge of the village, then marched on the market in single file. By now nearly all the Kom women had joined the movement; many came from other villages. They wore hats fashioned of dried plantain leaves, fiber skirts, and loincloths similar to the men's. Over their shoulders were draped the Anlu vines. Each woman carried a stout staff with which she rapped any poor unsuspecting man who happened to get in her way. All morning they jostled and shoved, publicly ridiculing the culprit by dancing and singing mocking songs. No buying or selling was possible. The chief sent enchindas, carrying branches of the sacred shrub that was his special emblem. Despite their orders and threats, the women persisted in their actions, and it was impossible to restore order.

Each week they descended on the transgressor's compound, draped it with vines and tendrils, and overturned his gourds. Sometimes they contaminated his cooking pots with garden eggs, which would cause him to become thin and sick; now and then they defiled his compound and urinated in the storage vessels. They were convinced that Beluh would capitulate in a few weeks, particulary because his wife had joined Anlu and refused to feed him. But Beluh was a stubborn one. He lived on fruits and dried corn that he cooked himself, and in this way, he flaunted public opinion for over two months.

At last, however, thin and tired of it all, he was persuaded by his friends to surrender. Draping the Anlu vines around his neck, he went to the leader's compound. She called the Anlu women together. With them was Fen, ready to face him and receive his apology. Beluh and his friends had brought the requisite number of goats, fowl, and palm oil, which he was directed to deliver to Fen's hut.

The leader and her helpers stripped Beluh of the vines and the loincloth he wore and escorted him, naked, to the nearby river. There they bathed him and immersed his entire body in the stream. His cooking pots, sullied by the rancid garden eggs, were washed clean. He was carried back to his own compound. The women rubbed him with powdered camwood mixed with palm oil, put a fresh fiber cloth over his loins, and fed him a nourishing stew. It was the ritual bathing that removed the guilt. After this, the incident was not mentioned again.

Ingwa was aghast. He had never seen anything like it. He had heard of Anlu, but in Bafut, where the Fon ruled with determined authority, it could never have been invoked. Indeed, it seemed to have been only in Kom that it was used at all (in historical times) and then only rarely. Several Bukum told him that during their lifetime they had seen it only once or twice before.*

Nearly three years later a small delegation from Bafut passed through Kom on its way to another funeral; this time they were going far over the mountains in the eastern end of the grasslands. They came out of their way to pick up Ingwa, for again he was to be the Fon's representative. The group lingered in Kom for several days, resting and feasting. To pay for Ingwa's sojourn, the Bafut men brought guns, ammunition, ivory, beads, cowrie shells, gorgeous Jukun cloths, and a Toby jug. There was also a lovely young girl who had been captured in a recent raid.

As the men returned to Bafut, Ndi, Ingwa's half-brother, joined them at Babanki. Chunga had returned several months before. The two young men traded stories and jokes about their exile. Ingwa was nearly as strongly attached to Ndi as he was to Chunga. He promised himself that if he were chosen to succeed Aboumbi, he would select Ndi to serve in the place of honor on his left, because he had planned already to give Chunga the place of equal rank and privilege on the right.

* During the recent struggle for independence, in 1958–59, this same movement was so twisted by a few politicians that it degenerated into a technique of political persecution.

Number-One Wife

World War I had ended before Ingwa returned from exile. The Bafut he knew had started to change slightly. The larger territory of the Cameroons was no longer in German hands. The Treaty of Versailles awarded one tenth of the area, including the Bamenda grasslands, to England and the remaining nine tenths to France. Although British troops had been in charge since 1917, it was not until 1922 that England received her mandate from the League of Nations. Because this new territory was so small, about seven hundred miles long and averaging only fifty miles in width, the northern strip was incorporated into the adjacent province of Northern Nigeria. The southern portion became the separate province of Southern Nigeria. This made for easier administration, despite the fact that at the conference table tribal and ethnic lines had been severed with little regard for the constituents.

The theory of indirect rule was well established in the British West African colonies, and the new mandated area profited from it. It was introduced in Nigeria around 1900 by Sir Frederick (later Lord) Lugard, the British colonial administrator. By the standards of the day, he was the most enlightened official on the continent. For reasons of economy and common sense, Lugard recognized the existing local administrations, realizing that many tribal affairs could be left in their hands. His practice of allowing the emirs and sultans to retain the reigns of autonomy slowly gained favor with other British administrators. With penetrating insight, this unusual man insisted that tribal life could and should be developed to equip the Africans for the larger life of the colony.

Lord Lugard convinced his superiors in England that the idea of indirect rule was economically advantageous. Because it followed so closely the era of humanitarianism that had swept Europe in the previous fifty years, many of his countrymen were amenable to his advanced ideas. The traders and a few administrators grumbled at first. But they discovered that a stable colony, free from constant bloodshed and internecine wars, provided a safer and more fertile environment for trade.

The Native Authority Courts were given considerable powers and official status. In the handling of civil and criminal cases, the British district officer became an adviser rather than the judge. The chiefs and their councils were given executive responsibilities, with power to make bylaws and see that they were obeyed. They levied local taxes and used the money for the benefit of the people. In the main, tribal customs were left intact, except for such institutions as slavery and ritual cannibalism. These were stamped out wherever possible. The native rulers received a yearly stipend to compensate, somewhat, for their added expenses. In return, they were to collect and deliver the taxes and provide men for military, police, and labor services.

Ingwa and Ndi returned to Bafut as it was entering the difficult period of adjustment to a new administration. For those who were willing to try, there was now another European language to learn. Once more, a few strange customs were imposed over the traditional ones. The German mission schools and churches were taken over by English and Swiss missionaries. A Roman Catholic mission requested permission to build in Bafut. Soon the young men were learning the precise diction of British speech, in addition to the pidgin English some of them, traders mostly, had been using for years. Several Bafut warriors had fought under the German flag and had returned with German army–issue clothing; except for their wounds, this was all some of them received for their services.

Ingwa was a bit heavier now than before his sojourn in Kom, yet his liveliness and boisterousness had not diminished. As he and Ndi neared the village, they saw the thatched roof of the majestic Achum, an awesome symbol of the divine power that protected the people. They both shouted aloud. The older men smiled indulgently; they recognized signs of homesickness.

By the time the travelers arrived, a large crowd had gathered in the king's compound. The gifts from Kom were studied with shrewd appraisal. There were no slaves, because the Europeans frowned mightily on slavery. Instead there were the usual carved ivory tusks, smaller ivory trinkets, wooden masks burnished with red camwood, carved stools, guns, and ammunition. There were shell beads from the coast and beads of European manufacture, as well as the famous woven cloth of Kom.

Then came the speeches. The elders reported that both Ingwa and Ndi had justified the Fon's faith in them and were worthy representatives of Bafut. Chunga was there, having returned just three days earlier from Bande. As the three young men listened to the cheers of welcome, there seemed to be no reason now for jealousy on the part of any of their brothers. The identity of the Fon's successor was still a well-kept secret. It would remain so while Aboumbi enjoyed excellent health. During these festivities, Ingwa visited with Ashoh. She pointedly asked him about his interest in the opposite sex, but he laughed shyly and told her he was still looking.

After the evening's celebration, Ingwa slept in the military house. He was so full of palm wine he neither knew nor cared what condition his own hut was in. When he investigated, in the morning, he found that one of his young cousins, Fontwi, had been using it. Fontwi was a homely little fellow to whom Ingwa took a fancy. He was shorter than many of the Bafut, but exceedingly strong. Down one side of his face ran an ugly scar, the result of a headlong tumble out of a palm tree after his fiber belt had broken. An excellent musician, he was full of good humor and high spirits. Ingwa wanted to repay the youth for taking care of his hut. Impulsively, he asked Fontwi to stay and share the two rooms. The youth was delighted; this meant that he would not have the immediate expense of building his own hut. Because he admired Ingwa tremendously, he gladly seized this chance to learn from the older man.

All of them now settled down to the methodical life of Bafut. Ingwa reported to the king each day. Fontwi took over the marketing of palm products. When the work became too much for one man, he recruited half-brothers and cousins from their lineage to help. Ingwa, Chunga, and Ndi formed a triumvirate in the court, taking turns on the many excursions to Banso, the Ndop plain, or the British headquarters in Bamenda. Ingwa was vaguely aware of changes in the government offices at Bamenda, but under the strong authority of the king and the Bukum, the affairs of the Bafut tribe ran smoothly. The young prince remained absorbed with his own life.

With his return from Kom, he began to take more notice of the young women and girls. One soft, warm evening he walked home with Chunga. They had helped a friend arrange a funeral service. It was the kind of night when young men everywhere talk about their sweethearts. Chunga had made his choice; he was to be married within the month. Now he chided Ingwa for remaining single.

Ingwa laughed. "I must wait until you are married. Then I'll send you to the girl's father to speak for me."

They both chuckled. The intermediary Chunga had sent to present his case had been nearly bowled over, so anxious was the father to marry his daughter to a prince. She was equally willing, too, so her bride price was not exorbitant.

Even a Fon's son was required to pay the age-old compensation to a man for the loss of a worker in his household. If the daughter objected to the suitor and her father respected her feelings, the bride price was raised. Occasionally, this discouraged the suitor. But if, against her wishes, the father and the girl's maternal uncle concurred on the price, there was little she could do but consent. Many fathers had discovered, however, that this initial compliance by the girl meant less trouble later on, and so a man generally took his daughter's feelings into account. If not, her only recourse was to marry, but stir up such trouble and dissension in her husband's compound that he was forced to divorce her and send her back to her father. In that instance, the bride price was not refunded. If she remarried, however, her new husband paid the bride price, and the father then turned it over to the first man. When a husband beat his wife severely, without cause, she could return to her father's compound, and no remittance was necessary.

There was an old story about a girl who refused to marry the man her father had chosen. Rigorously beaten by her parents, she was dragged to the man's compound three times. Each time she ran away, screaming, "You cannot force me to stay." Finally, rather than submit to this marriage that she abhorred, she hanged herself from a tree. The man could not regain his bride price. Usually, however, the girl ran away from her village rather than enter into a marriage she hated. If she was lucky, she found someone more to her liking. A good worker was nearly always acceptable in a household.

Lack of children was another reason for divorce. The father arranged for the wife (his daughter) to consult a diviner. If, after certain recommendations, there were still no children, the marriage was dissolved. Then, because the onus lay upon the husband, no refund was forthcoming. But in some instances, the wife remained with her husband, especially if he had other wives and children. Because she had fewer responsibilities, she often traded in the market each week. Children of divorce remained with the father. If they were not yet weaned, the mother took them with her, but she returned them later to their father. Life for an unmarried woman was extremely difficult, and spinsters were rare in Bafut. Most girls hoped to marry men who would be kind, give them children, and not force them to work too hard. With the polygynous system of marriage, there were always co-wives to help with the work, succor one during childbirth, and cooperate on the farms. As in most societies around the world, the women generally accepted their portions, and misfits were not frequent.

At the funeral ceremonies he and Chunga had helped to arrange, Ingwa noticed that one of the young girls shyly glanced his way. She was dancing with the sisters of the dead man. Like them, she was clad only in a fiber skirt. Funeral ceremonies did not show women to their advantage, yet, in spite of the mourning ashes smeared on her forehead, there was a tantalizing air about her. She had a pleasant, though not beautiful, face. Her body, as she moved in the mourning dance, was smooth and supple. Ingwa sensed a soothing quality in her. It was as though she were saying, "See, I have had experience with death and I could comfort you in all things."

Later, at the feast, she passed him fruit. As she leaned over him, one of her breasts lightly touched his shoulder. He turned to look into her eyes, and he felt the blood flushing into his cheeks and a thundering in his ears. Her smooth upper arm had a small circle of little scars, the result of her initiation into womanhood.

He stared at her face, her eyes, her arms. Finally, Chunga, sitting next to him, poked him in the ribs and tittered,

"Take some fruit, Ingwa. Don't be so slow!"

Ingwa murmured something under his breath and turned back to the roistering men.

That night he determined to learn more about the girl. Her name, he knew, was Shumba. Her father, Mako, was quarterhead of an outlying ward and a member of the Bukum. Ingwa knew him and liked him. He thought Mako would be amenable to the idea of Shumba marrying a son of the Fon. But what about the girl? What about the Fon?

When Ingwa approached his father on the subject, Aboumbi grinned at him. He told Ingwa several men had offered him one of their daughters. But the Fon thought it best for Ingwa to make his own choice. Fortunately, Shumba was not from the same lineage, so there would be no conflict there. Aboumbi promised Ingwa that he wanted to give him his first wife. If Shumba was the girl Ingwa wanted, financial arrangements would be made at once.

The Fon was true to his word. A few days later, Muma and one of the Council of Elders were sent to visit Mako. The two men carried a large calabash of palm wine. Mako was quite taken aback. Shumba was not considered his most marriageable daughter, but he surmised she would not oppose it. When she heard the news, later, she was overjoyed. There had been few overtures of this kind that were to her liking. She had observed Ingwa about the village and at several ceremonies. At the funeral feast she knew he had noticed her. That he was the Fon's son impressed her, but not unduly. Many royal princes were said to be over-bearing, proud, and overly fond of palm wine. Some were lazy, a characteristic repugnant to the Bafut. Ingwa had a reputation for kindness and dignity. His sense of humor was well known. From her father Shumba had heard of Ingwa's comportment while he was in exile. She told her father she would be content to become Ingwa's wife.

Muma and the elder came again. This time several enchindas carried a fifty-pound bag of salt and several gourds of palm oil. The salt, as good as money, was a little friendly persuasion for

Mako's wives. They were overjoyed with the gift. Shumba's mother was ecstatic. Immediately, she began to make plans for the wedding feast; she even forgot to ask her husband how large the bride price would be. But her brother, Shumba's uncle, was alert enough on that score. He told Mako to set a high price, because Ingwa, or, in fact, the Fon, could afford to pay. By the acceptance of these initial gifts, Shumba's acquiescence was assured. Final negotiations were then begun.

When Ingwa brought the first installment, Shumba's uncle and her grandfather, Mako's father-in-law, were invited to receive their traditional share of the payment. It consisted of two large calabashes of palm oil, a gun and ammunition, and a small bag of beads. Ingwa also brought a lovely bead, intriguingly carved, which he asked Mako to give Shumba. They had not seen each other since the day of the funeral feast.

Mako accepted the first payment, then ordered one of his wives to fetch Shumba. She scurried out and returned in a twinkling, leading the girl by the hand. The mother was close behind. The three women filed in and stood with their heads bowed. Mako explained that Ingwa, a son of the Fon, had come to give the first payment on her bride price. As he asked if she was content with such an arrangement, the girl looked at her father shyly, then lowered her head. Her father asked, again, if she were willing to become Ingwa's wife. A light spread slowly over her face, and an incredibly sweet smile parted her lips. Ingwa thought she was lovely.

"Yes, father, I am content." She spoke in a voice so low that Ingwa heard only the last word. Then she turned her head down once more. Mako was more than pleased. He held out Ingwa's bead, which the girl received as though in a trance. Mako told the mother that Ingwa had brought salt. When the women left the hut, there was a swishing out in the yard, as the other wives and their children, who could not resist eavesdropping, hurried out of the way.

The men settled down to make arrangements for the final payments. Because the Fon had given Ingwa the bride price, there was no need to delay longer than was necessary for the preparations. Sometimes the groom worked for months and even years to pay the price asked by a greedy father. Ingwa also knew that many village girls, in violation of the more traditional Bafut custom, visited their future husbands before they were married.

Bisi, for example, his uncle's wife, had done this, Ingwa knew. On various special occasions, several times before they were married, she had taken her future husband a small gift from her mother. She had remained with him a few days, cooking for him and sleeping with him. Then she had returned to her mother, bearing a small exchange present from her husband-to-be. But this pattern was rarely followed by royal males.

In the old days, if a man was found with a girl to whom he was not married, both of them were killed. This taboo was rigorously upheld. If the wife of a king committed adultery, both she and her lover were killed. More recently, this had been modified so that the couple was merely banished from Bafut.

Ingwa was content to wait for Shumba until they were married. But he was too restless to build a new house immediately; instead, he asked Fontwi to move out. It was to be a temporary arrangement, for the young prince planned to build a compound in his own grove of palm trees.

Shumba's mother, meanwhile, was busily rounding up her relatives to help with the wedding feast. There were plantains and other fruits to be collected, as well as cocoyams, red peppers, kola nuts, ground nuts, palm oil, and palm wine. Meat was procured, cooked, and dried so that there would be enough for stews. Because fresh meat was not always available, a live goat was saved for the important day. Ingwa was expected to provide plantains and palm wine, as well as brass manilla money—armlets —for each of Shumba's sisters. The amounts were carefully calculated by Mako as part of the wedding settlement. Ingwa vividly remembered the wedding feast of one of his friends. The final celebration was delayed because the bride's mother demanded extra payment. Her future son-in-law had passed her on the path while she was carrying a heavy load from her farm. He had refused to help her, and for that insult she demanded extra money. The ensuing palaver took the better part of the day and postponed the feast. Ingwa knew that a "mother-in-law must be handled as carefully as a calabash of palm oil." He took special care to be gallant to all of Shumba's family, so there was no such delay.

On the day of the wedding, Shumba, her mother, and all the mother's sisters came to the compound of Ingwa's uncle. They were carrying vast quantities of food. As was the custom, Mako was not present, and his place was taken by Shumba's maternal uncle, fulfilling his role as her "second" father. Shumba's grandfather and the rest of the family came, filling the spacious yard with their friendly, noisy shouts of goodwill. The Fon was not there, because he had been called away to the Ndop plain. Ashoh, Ingwa's two sisters, and a few aunts arrived. Immediately they began to help the bride's female relatives prepare the feast.

First the men of the wedding party were fed, then the friends and other relatives, and finally the women and children received their share. The palm wine was bountiful, and it quickly lubricated the tongues of the speech makers. All his friends were there, along with Kimi, Chunga, and Fontwi. Ndi and Ingwa's bachelor friends regaled the crowd with ribald stories of what opportunities Ingwa had passed up. The bride's uncle, on behalf of her family, exhorted the groom to treat Shumba well. Everyone wished the happy pair long life and many children. This took up most of the afternoon. When the drums began, everyone joined in the dancing. Not until darkness crept over the blue mountains and down along the village paths did the wedding guests slowly and reluctantly take their departure. Because there were so many of them, and because the palm wine flowed so freely, it was late before the compound quieted down.

Then, in traditional fashion, two of Ingwa's sisters and his female cousins took charge of the bride. She still could not go to Ingwa. Instead, she stayed with his sisters during the night. Pleasant, cheerful young women they were, with families of their own. They had a strong affection for their brother. In the morning, after they had cooked the plantain Ingwa provided, they carefully washed Shumba and rubbed her nubile young body with palm oil until it was glossy. All the while they instructed her in matters pertaining to sex and family responsibilities. She had heard it all from her mother, but she listened respectfully and promised to be a good wife.

For a week Ingwa's sisters and cousins groomed Shumba. They fed her and pampered her. Finally they arrayed her in new strings of beads around her hips, placed new rings in her ear lobes, and triumphantly led her back to her father's compound. Here all her family waited to embrace her.

"See how well we have treated your daughter," said Ingwa's older sister. "You need have no fears for her while she is Ingwa's wife. She will not want. Already she is much fatter than a week ago. In addition, she has been learning what is necessary to make Ingwa a happy husband and father."

The sisters escorted the bride back to Ingwa's hut. Two older women in the compound took her to Ingwa and stayed with the bridal couple until they were certain they knew exactly what to do. Then the women withdrew, leaving Ingwa and Shumba alone at last.

Have Mercy on This House

The marriage was an auspicious one for the young princ
Shumba proved to be an excellent farmer. She was a diligent a
resourceful worker. Her obedience, patience, and humility e
deared her to the tiny community within the compound. O
of her little cousins, a diminutive girl of nearly eight, came to li
with them for the first few months. It was her duty to a
Shumba with the cooking, carry water, bring firewood, and he
in the fields. This left Shumba with the freedom and energy
satisfy her young husband. They were a sprightly, vivacio
couple, always vigorous and cheerful and full of gentle teasi
When he imbibed too heavily of palm wine, she used her wiles
lure him back to their hut. Ingwa planned to build his own co
pound, but his uncle begged him to stay. Shumba, in turn, h
become devoted to her ready-made family. The little cousin
turned to her mother about six months later, and Shumba th
took full charge of her household.

The threads of market days, hunting expeditions, funera
births, and weddings lent color to the fabric of their lives. Wh
Shumba discovered, to her deep satisfaction, that she was pre
nant, she subtly intimated that it was time Ingwa took anoth
wife. Another woman could help her farm and assist in t
chores around the compound and, most important, keep h
sexually satisfied. After the baby was born, she would not ha
intercourse with him for two years, perhaps longer—as was co
mon in many West African tribes; plenty of mother's milk w
essential for a strong, healthy child. Shumba knew it would be
her advantage to have a co-wife of whom she approved rat
than wait for Ingwa to make his own choice. Ingwa, in tu
realized that if she had someone in mind, he could trust h

Peace among the wives in the compound was essential if there was to be happiness and prosperity.

Following Shumba's lead, Ingwa asked if she had someone in mind.

The girl hesitated, while she carefully applied some red camwood to her forehead and cheeks. Tikar mothers-to-be had done this from time immemorial while waiting for their babies; many young women wore it while nursing a baby. Little nursemaids sometimes wore red masks of camwood while caring for their tiny charges.

Finally, she told him that if she didn't suggest someone, his mother or sisters would pick a second wife for him. She told him about Mankana, the daughter of her father's brother. The girl was not too young, a good worker, and attractive. She was interested in Ingwa, too; she had confided as much to Shumba. Ingwa laughed uproariously; he realized his wife would flatter him to the extreme in order to gain her point. Shumba smiled. She was fond of Mankana, a lively, intelligent, and articulate girl. She knew they would get on well together. Besides, if Ingwa hesitated too long, someone else was certain to offer the father a good bride price. The next day Ingwa sent Fontwi to talk to the girl's father.

With the arrival of Shumba's baby—a boy—and the addition of a second wife, Ingwa decided it was time for him to build a more spacious compound of his own. He discussed the situation with his uncle, Fontwi, and Chunga. Between them they found enough men of their lineage to help build three huts and enclose them all with a handsome fiber fence. There was to be a house for Ingwa, one for Shumba and her baby, and one for Mankana and the children she was certain to have. Shumba was beside herself with joy. She had feared she would have to share a two-room hut with Ingwa's new wife. As a son of the king, Ingwa already had accrued prestige and wealth; many wives were bound to follow. Even as the senior wife, Shumba would have to share more crowded quarters as the compound grew. It would be pleasant to be alone as long as possible.

Ingwa's hut was the first to be completed. About twelve feet square, it was constructed of raffia palm poles and plastered thickly with mud the women carried up from the stream. Over the pointed pole roof a thick, fragrant thatch of elephant grass was laid by a professional thatcher. The men worked several weeks. When they had finished, there were two rooms, with a storage area between the ceiling and the roof. A raffia-pole bed was built on the right side of the door. About four feet above the ground were racks to hold Ingwa's possessions. Windows were unnecessary, for nights in Bafut were cool and everyone spent the days outdoors. The threshold was about a foot and a half high, to keep out snakes and high water during the rains. The wooden door frame was elaborately carved with the customary stylized symbols of the Tikar people: lizards, spiders, the bush cow, and the leopard. The sliding door of raffia poles could easily be pushed aside. Later, after a daily fire had warmed the mud walls so they dried to a fine hardness, a second ceiling would be built beneath the first. This would provide storage space and a drying rack for corn, ground nuts, and palm kernels. Without a chimney, the smoke filtered through the mesh of thatching on the roof and provided a preservative for the produce stored on the rack. Shumba planned to live in one of the two rooms until her own hut was finished.

Before they moved in, there was a gargantuan feast for all who had worked on the building. Ingwa provided a goat and the usual palm wine. The members of his lineage, including the Fon himself, came with gifts of cocoyams and fruit. An elegant old uncle of the Fon's, who was the "father of the lineage," officially blessed the house. He bore the same name as Ingwa's brother: Ndi.

"Now that Ingwa has a house of his own, we know he will have good fortune." Old Ndi placed near the door a stone about six inches long. White and smooth it was from much washing and tumbling in Menchem Falls, the spiritual home of the dead chiefs.

In a deep, resonant voice Ndi went on: "In this stone rests the spirit of one of your grandfathers. We have brought him here to guard you and your family. He will protect you from sickness. He will give advice and comfort when you are at your wits' end. Never neglect to heed the voices of your ancestors!"

Ndi splashed the stone with a bit of palm wine from a cup, then handed the cup to Ingwa. After taking a sip, Ingwa spattered the sacred stone with wine and whispered, "Oh, grandfather, have mercy on this house."

He handed the wine back to Ndi. The Fon drank and also poured some wine on the stone. Each man in the circle did likewise, and when the cup once more came to Ndi, the old man chanted, "Blessings on this house!"

The men of the family went out into the spacious yard. Here the crowd waited impatiently for the food and fun. After the men were served, Shumba, the other women, and the children gathered around the great iron pot of hot pepper stew. On large banana leaves they placed a gray swirl of starchy fufu. Into the center hole was poured the spicy stew, and the leaves were then passed to the waiting throng. In turn, each person took a bit of fufu between his thumb and first two fingers, dipped it into the sharp red stew, and popped the whole into his mouth. Several men with razorlike knives of iron passed among the crowd, holding great chunks of roasted goat and cutting off a minute piece for each person. There was plenty of fruit. The men always carried horn cups for palm wine. The women and children merely cupped their hands and quickly gulped what wine they could, as the custodian of the calabash made his way among them. After they all had eaten and drunk, someone passed a gourd of water. Each one washed his hands and rinsed his mouth; the more fastidious took out little sticks and cleaned their teeth with the frayed ends.

The feasting, dancing, and singing consumed most of the afternoon. Finally, the guests started noisily down the paths to their homes. It had been a good party; the livelier the celebration, the more it reflected their approval of their host and his hospitality.

Before many months passed there were two more huts in the compound, and Mankana joined the family group. Her marriage followed the Bafut pattern. Shumba herself helped the women wash and oil the lovely bride during the week of preparation. After the marriage Shumba's younger sister came to live with Ingwa and Mankana for a few months to relieve the new bride of household drudgery.

In the spring of the year the mountains around Bafut were hazy with the dust of the harmattan, and the pall was compounded by the annual burning of the fields. Each January the men set fire to the tall elephant grass. This made it easier for the women to prepare their fields for agriculture. The soft haze lay motionless upon the landscape, not to be disturbed until the strong winds in the late spring. The first small rains, and finally the heavy rains, would wash it away in time. But now the sun was warm and tender; everyone was at peace with the world.

Fontwi, one morning, came striding into Ingwa's compound. The youth recently had finished his own hut. He was fast becoming an entrepreneur in the exportation of palm oil, and he sent his agents as far as Adamawa in the north and to Banyang in the south. In spite of his homely face and bandy legs, he had succeeded in making a good marriage and was casting about for another wife. Consistently, he was sought after as a musician. His business acumen was becoming legendary, and his cheerful, rollicking personality contributed to his popularity. With a broad grin, he asked for Ingwa.

Mankana sat before her hut with her week-old daughter on her lap. She was about to pierce the child's tiny earlobes with a sharp thorn from the base of a nearby palm tree. By pulling through a piece of fiber cord, she could keep the hole open until it healed. Then she would insert minute earrings, presents from Fontwi and his wife. Lazily, she looked up. Ingwa had gone to help his brother Boombi harvest the flying ants. They were out in the bush building the ant shelter.

As Fontwi left the compound, he passed Shumba's little boy leading a blind uncle into the yard. The boy and man each held tightly to opposite ends of a three-foot length of bamboo. In this way the blind man was fairly mobile. Because he was a good singer, he was always welcome throughout the village. Little Mako, named for his grandfather, occasionally received small amounts of salt for leading his blind uncle. Fontwi nodded approvingly to himself. Shumba's children were being imbued with her sense of kindness and sympathy for others.

He hurried out to the field, where he knew he would find Ingwa.

"Ho, Ingwa," shouted Fontwi. "How many baskets of ants will you sell me?" This was a great joke between them, for Ingwa had neither the time nor the inclination to work for long at this task. It was Fontwi who had done most of the work when they lived together, and now Boombi was taking over.

Each spring, for many years, the young men had set up two-foot fences around the anthills to trap the succulent white ants, or termites. The same hills were used by the same men year after year. When Fontwi arrived, a saucer-shaped space had already been dug between the fence and the gigantic anthill. Near the fence, the trench was a foot deep, nearly four feet long and about eight inches wide. The anthill itself and the ground surrounding it were being covered with palm leaves. It looked like a thatched hut with a small door, from which led the open trench.

After the first spring thunderstorm, the men would rush out to their anthill. The ditch would be full of the flying insects. Hearing the thunder, they were frightened into flying out, but the palm leaves prevented them from flying free. Helpless, they sank into the open trench. The men gathered them in large baskets and took them home. The women prepared them in a simple manner. Some were browned in a greaseless pan; some had their wings removed and were dried for stews.

The Bafut and other people of the grasslands were so hungry for this delicacy each spring that many ants were consumed before the men and boys returned to their homes. In order to insure a good crop for the following year, each man offered a few ants on a leaf to all members of his family. After the second harvest, many men sold their surplus ants in the market. Later in the summer, the same area often produced excellent mushrooms. These were dried, giving extra flavor to the stews.

Ingwa's broad face wrinkled with pleasure at seeing Fontwi. He retorted that he didn't think the younger man had come this distance just to get a few free ants. Fontwi agreed; he had come to ask for help in clearing another field for his wife to farm.

"You know, one hand cannot tie a bundle!" Fontwi loved to quote Bafut proverbs.

Boombi, the pragmatist, wondered if it wasn't too late. Fontwi said he thought that if the heavy rains held off a few more weeks, there would be time to put in some cocoyams, beans, and ground nuts. His wife needed the extra field for his widowed mother-in-law, who planned to live with them.

The three men arranged to help each other: Fontwi to assist with the ant harvest, and Ingwa and his brother to help clear the new field for farming. In this cooperative manner the male mem-

bers of a lineage could get extra help for tasks too difficult for a
man to do alone. In this way Ingwa's house had been finished. In
this way Fontwi now asked for help in his work.

After the men had staked out the area, they cut the heavy
elephant grass and the brush with their bush knives. These big,
heavy knives were usually fashioned by the local smiths. Some
came from the better smiths at Babanki. European knives had
filtered down to the markets from northern Africa as early as
1850. After the brush was burned, the women took over the
farming.

Land was life in the Cameroons. All the land in Bafut was
theoretically owned by the Fon, but for practical purposes, areas
were handed out to each family in the tribe to buy, sell, or farm
as they saw fit. Palm-tree products, the oil, kernels, and wine,
were marketed by the men. The farming was done by the
women, each one receiving plots of land, first from her father,
later from her husband. When she could no longer work the
land, it reverted to the person who had given it to her or to his
heir. It was to her advantage, of course, to have these areas near
each other and close to the village. But if they were widely separated, she often solved the problem by rotating her crops or even
allowing some plots to lie fallow.

Those women who devoted most of their time to agriculture
had as many as six farms, rotating their work monthly on each
one. The time a woman spent traveling to and from her plot
could, therefore, be considerable—as much as four to five hours a
day. However, the Tikar women had a real love for their land.
They never complained of the labor necessary to sustain it. They
were jealous, too, of their freedom to manage these farms as they
saw fit. The fertility of the women and the fertility of the land
were vital to the well-being of the Bafut tribe; the women were
as proud of their fields and their kitchen gardens as they were of
their innumerable children.

After the men cleared her field, Fontwi's wife, with her
short-handled hoe, scraped a few inches of arable red soil into a
pile over the mound of dried elephant grass. She left a tail of
grass at one end of each mound. When she finished the field,
there were regularly spaced mounds twelve feet long, four feet
wide, and three feet high, reaching from one end of the plot to

the other. She lit the tails of grass and allowed them to smolder in
the mounds for several days. This provided a minuscule amount
of fertilizer, so badly needed in the almost sterile soil. (Apparently the hot sun and the heavy tropical rains leach out many of
the nutrients from the soil.) A week or so later, when the fires
were burned out completely, Fontwi's wife planted in each
hillock a variety of crops: maize, sweet potatoes, beans,
cocoyams, and ground nuts.* A few weeks later she put some
calabash seeds among the growing plants. These were given careful attention. When the gourds were about five inches in
diameter, she set them upright to give them a flat base. By
harvesting them at intervals, she obtained a variety of sizes and
shapes. The calabash seeds she utilized by drying and cracking
them for stews.

After she had planted her calabash seeds, Fontwi's wife
stopped to visit with Mankana. The two young women were
about the same age and were genuinely fond of each other.
Mankana held up her tiny daughter, freshly bathed and oiled, so
the younger woman could inspect the earrings. The two of them
crowed and cooed over the child for some minutes, and then
Mankana gave the baby a breast. The younger girl watched with
longing, almost feeling the pull of the tiny mouth on her own
nipple. Her first pregnancy had ended in a miscarriage. She
hoped to become pregnant again soon, although, with another
wife about to come into the compound, it would take time.
Mankana noticed her friend's eyes darken wistfully. With tact
she managed to change the subject.

Through the rest of the afternoon they chattered, drowsy
with the sun and full of well-being. Before they separated, they
arranged to see a diviner about a fetish to protect their farms
against thieves.

The two women sauntered over to the diviner's hut the next
day. Each carried a small calabash of palm wine and a live fowl.
The fee varied according to the size of the fields, but this would
be a good start. For a while they sat and joked with the diviner.
He was a man in their quarter who, long ago, had been pressed
into service at the German fort in Bamenda. So clever was he that
during the year he had spent with the Europeans he had always

* Today the Bafut women usually practice single-crop agriculture.

been able to find others to labor for him, yet his record was good, and from his divining he made money on the side. He was popular with the entire tribe because the majority of his prognostications were borne out. In one corner of his yard sat a pot with a broken bottom. This was the spider's prison. The diviner kept the creature well fed, but by placing this pot over the burrow, he was assured of the spider's presence when it was needed.

He greeted the women with a sly smile. "I am surprised that the wife of the great Ingwa and the wife of Fontwi, mighty trader in palm oil, should find it necessary to come to me for a fetish."

The women giggled appreciatively at this. Just then, a slight young fellow danced into the yard. He was pulling a wooden food tray, with a squealing small boy perched on top. These were two of the diviner's children, so separated in age as to be man and boy, but so near each other emotionally and mentally that they could have been twins. The older boy, a youth of about twenty, was the firstborn child of the diviner's second wife, a foolish woman who never turned her face to the wall when she heard Kweyifon's bells—unlike the villagers, who used to say, "A person's back can't see juju."

When her baby was born, he seemed to be normal, but his mind had never kept up with his body. "He lives in a different world," the people said, but they tempered their treatment of him with kindness. They teased him and laughed at his foolish remarks. The children loved him and regarded him as one of themselves. The younger child was about five; he quivered with excitement as they came roaring around the corner. Protruding nearly three inches from his round little potbelly was an umbilical hernia, all too common a sight in the grasslands and other parts of West Africa.

The diviner smiled serenely when he saw his two boys; the women laughed good-humoredly at their antics. Indulgently, they poured palm wine for the youngsters, who drank it thirstily from cupped hands. Then the compound echoed with laughter as the foolish one pretended to be drunk, cavorting as a court jester would before the king. Vigorously, he danced. Then, grinning happily, he squatted down before them to receive their acclaim. His head was too large for his fragile body. His teeth glistened white against his ebony skin. His eyes, black as velvet, gazed wit-lessly into their faces. The father ordered him to get more palm wine for the women. While the young man went to find his mother, the diviner cradled the younger child between his knees, caressing one shining shoulder with love and tenderness.

For some time the women conversed about everything from the weather to the state of the Fon's health to the European school run by schoolmaster Shu. Finally, they broached the rea-son for their visit: a fetish to protect their crops from thieves.

The diviner stared intently at the two women, who anx-iously awaited his decision. Just then, the foolish one returned to the yard with a gourd of palm wine. The diviner held up one fin-ger, as though testing the wind, then offered them more refreshment. He decided they would profit by installing a fetish over their fields. He went into his hut and came back carrying two small, seedy-looking, dark fiber bags. They were decorated with colored beads, and bits of animal hair hung down the seams. He handed one to each woman.

"Hang these from a long pole placed diagonally at the entrance to your farms," he said. "They will protect the fields from thieves and insure a good harvest. Anyone who steals yams from a field with this fetish over it will surely fall dead."

After pronouncing this dire prediction, he graciously ac-cepted the fowls the women proffered. Later, each one would bring him a small share of her harvest. They hurried out to their fields and fastened the fetishes onto long, raffia-palm poles. These they dug into the ground so that the entrances would be guarded. Then, satisfied, the women trudged slowly back to their homes.

A Sacred Pool Is Violated

The British administrative officers made no secret of the fact that they considered Aboumbi one of the most responsible paramount chiefs in the grasslands. They heartily endorsed the traditional method by which he trained his sons for the future. The British practice of indirect rule proved fortunate for both sides. The Fon continued to rule the tribe in his usual autocratic manner.

Ingwa and Chunga were in their forties now. Both of them had several wives and many children. They were rich men, by Bafut standards, and they commanded enormous prestige and respect. Chunga had developed a temper that he sometimes found difficult to check. But his wives, Ingwa, or other friends would cajole and coax him into a better mood. The lives of both men were still in jeopardy, but by this time they had lived with the threat for so long that they seldom thought of danger. Ingwa appeared to have inherited his father's stubbornness and despotic manner; he ruled his compound fairly but sternly. Shumba found herself siding with her younger co-wives in more than one ticklish situation.

For some time the Fon had been represented by these two sons in important cases at the administrative office in Bamenda. Now, at the rear of a returning delegation, the two men discussed the events of their latest trip. Most of the men, including Ndi, Kimi, and Neba, hurried to reach home, for a storm was imminent and they knew it could be a bad one. They could hear rain in the distance, gentle and quiet at first, like the small sound of a distant waterfall. As it came closer, it increased to a driving, constant outpouring of water; it gushed noisily down the ditches along the road, taking with it all manner of debris, branches, brush, unswept food from the day's market, pebbles, and seeds. It also washed away much of the valuable topsoil.

Ingwa noted that the rains were early, that this should be but a shower, yet it seemed that Menchem Falls had been let loose. They both smiled ruefully, remembering sadder days when they had journeyed with the rest of the tribe to the great falls, where they had implored the ancestors for guidance during the days of their exile.

Darkness fell over the land. Then came the lightning, cutting great swathes of brightness across the mountains, trailing horrendous thunderclaps. In the blackness, as in a closed room, the men moved along cautiously and fearfully, swallowing water with every step, touching each other now and then to assure themselves they were still together. The noise of the rain and thunder prevented talking. There was no light, only intermittent illumination from the flashes of lightning.

At last they reached Ingwa's compound. Because it was too dangerous for him to continue alone, Chunga decided to remain here for the night. A tiny, smoky fire was burning in the main hut. Fastidiously, the men rubbed themselves dry. Shumba entered with hot food and a gourd of palm wine. Her face reflected her pleasure at their safe return, for she worried about her husband during these terrible storms. He told her that Chunga would stay until morning, that the storm was too wild for him to go on. Then he remarked that surely the witches must be abroad tonight. Mankana came in with more food. After the men had eaten and lit their pipes, Shumba queried them about the week's journey.

Chunga answered that all had gone very well indeed. He knew that Ingwa often discussed village affairs with his two older wives, for both of them were level-headed and extremely intelligent. The men related the details of their trip, they spoke of the friends they had seen, they described how they had cleverly trapped the British district officer into doing exactly what they, the Bafut, wished. All of them laughed hilariously at this trickery, realizing that the British officer probably was well aware of their conniving.

Then Ingwa asked his wives about the market. Every eighth day, for the Tikar observed an eight-day week, a weekly market was held in Bafut. In order to buy and sell, people from the surrounding territory trudged as far as twenty miles. On the other seven days of the week, the market was held in other villages or larger towns strategically located, so that the entire Bafut area was served by a large market every eight days and by little village stalls in the interim.

Everyone attended these weekly markets. They came to buy, to sell, to see and be seen, and to satisfy that seemingly inherent instinct for sociability. News and announcements from the king were given in the afternoon by old Kweyifon. Dressed in his fiber hood and clanging his spear, he was usually accompanied by several Bukum. His remarks were always prefaced by a recitation of the names of the ancestor chiefs. Then, in the name of the living Fon, Aboumbi, the announcements were given. This officially closed the market.

Separate "streets" were set aside for certain items. Palm products were sold in one area. The abattoir, or meat department, was always situated in one place, lending its stench to an already odoriferous air. In another street, hand-regulated Singer sewing machines were run by the men. Here arrangements could be made for a new Cameroons gown if a man could not, or did not wish to, fashion one himself. They were expensive, so if he could not afford a new one, a man had his old one mended. In their subsistence economy, however, few men possessed the equivalent of ten to twelve dollars for a gown with the requisite embroidery,* so many of them made their own. There was a street for knickknacks brought in by Hausa traders from the north; here were sold needles, thread, cotton cloth, knives, and pipes from England, tinware from Germany and Holland, beads and silver Maria Theresa dollars from Austria.

The little huts where palm wine was sold by the drink were soon crowded. The moment the men sold their goods, they came in out of the sun or rain to drink and chat with old friends. Sometimes an enterprising proprietor asked a few friends to bring their instruments, and by early afternoon music mingled with the hummings and buzzings of the market place.

The women earned additional income through selling corn fufu and other ground meal and fruits and vegetables from their

* By 1964 the price had risen to nearly sixty American dollars. It was a little cheaper if the customer furnished the material.

farms. Proudly they arranged the produce in colorful, symmetrical piles and pyramids. With their profits they bought salt and English cottons, which were becoming popular. Women also sold baskets in the crafts area. Nearly all other craft items, such as the Cameroons caps, fiber hats, shoulder bags, and scabbards for the knives, were made by the men. Traders brought in the iron bush knives made by smiths from other villages. Steel knives and cutlasses from Sheffield and Birmingham, England, enjoyed a continuing popularity. Even the children brought items to trade, the boys receiving small amounts of salt in return for cotton they gathered below the kapok trees. Although the German mark or the British pound and shilling had been the currency for some time, and people had the opportunity of becoming adjusted to the coins, there was always a preference for the traditional barter system. Even today, especially in less accessible areas, trading is still carried on in large measure through barter.

The market got under way early in the morning, supervised by a sanitary officer and his two assistants. They inspected all foodstuffs and destroyed any food they considered unfit for consumption. Any palm wine not up to standard was poured out on the ground. The men directed and regulated the market area in the morning and policed it during the day. By late afternoon the market was usually a squalid, filthy mess, foul-smelling from unsold fruit and meat, littered with debris and animal residue. The officers rounded up their corps of men to clean up everything for another week. After the Native Authority was introduced, a market supervisor was appointed in each division. It was his additional duty to collect the nominal rent for permanent stalls; vendors in the open did not pay rent. Although the Banso market attracted the largest number of people in the grassland area, the Bafut market served well over three thousand people each week.

Shumba's face was troubled as she told the men of the excitement they had missed. Glancing now and then at Mankana for corroboration, she told the story succinctly. Bisi, the wife of Ingwa's uncle, had rushed into the market about noon, screaming at the top of her voice. She was followed by nearly a dozen of the Fon's wives, Ashoh among them. No one could understand what she was crying about. Finally, her boy twin, the son who was about to become an enchinda, ran into the market after her.

Weeping and wailing, Bisi told Shumba she had tried to get some water from the Fon's private spring because she was tired of trudging down to the stream.

"Bisi always was an independent woman," chuckled Ingwa, remembering that years ago she had wormed from her husband a promise of education for this same boy. She knew perfectly well that no one but the Fon's wives was allowed to draw water from that spring. Wasn't the taboo sign on the path? Didn't that frighten her?

"Trouble never rings a bell," said Mankana darkly, quoting a Bafut proverb. "Tell them the rest, Shumba."

Bisi filled her gourds with water and was about to go up the path, when she slipped and fell back into the spring. Chunga tittered that it served her right.

The Fon's spring was taboo to everyone except his wives and daughters. Each spring those wives who wished to conceive went to bathe in its soothing coolness, for the sacred spring would bring fertility to the tribe as well as to the lush red earth. To violate the Fon's spring was an extremely serious offense.

As Bisi was climbing out, two of the royal wives came down the path and saw her. Immediately they started berating her, hurling sticks and stones, calling on their co-wives to come and help them. Bisi started to run home, but they cut her off and forced her to run into the market. There, they knew, the story would soon be known to everyone in the tribe.

Finally Bisi was able to break away, and with her little son at her heels, she escaped to her own compound. The market, of course, was in an uproar for the rest of the day. When Kweyifon came to deliver the Fon's weekly message to the people, he was accompanied by the entire Council of Elders. Visibly perturbed, he gave an unusually long speech about the sacred pool. Over and over, he reminded the people that no one was to go near it except those whom the king sanctioned, his wives, and his daughters. The king was enraged because the hallowed spring had been defiled. He issued orders for special meetings of the secret societies to ward off any sickness that might result.

The two men looked at each other in horror, remembering Ingwa's idle remark, earlier, that it was a night when witches must be abroad.

The vehement storm continued until nearly midnight. It filled the skies with thunder; it emptied its clouds upon an already saturated land. In the morning, just as a murky dawn was breaking, the signal drum* boomed its message to the entire tribe. This colossal, slit-log drum, over six feet long, was carved out of a single tree trunk. In its own hut, it lay in splendor at one end of the dance plaza. Only a few of the best drummers were permitted to beat out messages, information not always understood by all the people who heard it. Certain men in each quarter interpreted the meaning, then sent messengers throughout their wards. The people were commanded to remain in their compounds that entire day; no farming was allowed, for fear that Bisi's indiscretion might influence the crops. The Bukum planned to travel immediately to the sacred ancestor pool to ascertain the best way of counteracting this appalling deed.

As soon as they heard the drum, Ingwa and Chunga rushed over to the Fon's compound to see what they could do. There they found the Bukum, with Kweyifon already dressed in his fiber hood, ready to commence the long journey to Menchem Falls. During the absence of the Bukum no farming would be permitted. That night there was singing and drumming throughout the Bafut tribe. Ingwa and all his wives stayed late at the palace, helping the Fon ward off the pestilence that would undoubtedly come as a result of Bisi's foolishness. Already, the medicine society was preparing sacred ropes, impregnated with medicinal leaves to repel the sickness. These were spread across the paths leading out of the village.

Ingwa's uncle was so angry with his favorite wife that, fond though he was of her, he gave her a terrible beating. She lay huddled in a corner of her hut, whimpering loudly, a bundle of distress. Her co-wives were forbidden to go near her; she was attended only by her twin children, now about nine years old, the little boy and girl whom she had threatened to withhold from the Fon. There were two younger children, but they had been taken to another hut in the enclosure. Bisi was indeed a sad spectacle. Her eyes were swollen with weeping, her smooth body was bleeding where the whip had cut her flesh, her voice was so

* The drum by which only signals were sent. This was not the "talking drum" of the forest people.

hoarse she could scarcely speak. She had eaten nothing since the previous morning. Her wounds continued to bleed.

Shumba, though she knew the Fon would be furious if he found out, decided she must succor and comfort her friend as best she could. She knew the poor woman was alone, for the co-wives were too terrified to disobey their husband and the Fon. Although she was not royalty, Shumba, being the wife of a favored son, felt she could endure the Fon's wrath better than anyone else. Telling Mankana what she was about to do, she slipped out of the compound before sunup the next day.

For over a week Shumba stayed with the wretched Bisi. She bathed her and fed her, cared for her wounds, and calmed her fears. Ingwa wondered aloud where his wife had gone. Despite his noisy questions about her, Mankana declined to tell him. On the third day, when he visited Bisi's husband, he caught a glimpse of Shumba as she was pounding cocoyams for the children. He turned away quickly, preferring that she not see him. Secretly, however, he was proud of her, for he knew this was the kind of sympathy and loyalty he could expect if he ever needed it. He never told Mankana he had seen Shumba, nor did he tell his father who had helped to heal Bisi's wounds. The Fon was busy devising the proper punishment while waiting for the return of the council members with their report from the ancestor spirits.

A month after Bisi's rash act, Kweyifon and his men returned from Menchem Falls. Their spears jingled furiously as they passed through the village. They noted that little "toy" huts made of grass were standing in the paths that led to the various quarters. Around the huts, and hanging from their eaves, were minute straw figures. Already the people were trying to ward off sickness or bad luck of any kind. The elders nodded to each other in approval. After their report to the Fon and the rest of the Bukum, Bisi's fate would be announced in public.

Bisi, meanwhile, had recovered from her beating, but her fears increased when she realized her husband not only refused to encourage her but gave strict orders for no one, including her children, to go near her. He ignored Shumba, muttering loudly that evil would surely befall anyone who assisted his wretched wife. He threatened to divorce her, which meant she would be forced to return to her father's house, if that proud man would take her back. Bisi well knew that this was improbable. Because her bride price had been a large one and her husband could irrefutably ask for it to be refunded, it was not likely her father would be willing to pay for her indiscretion.

Shumba returned to her own compound, hoping to learn what the king and the Bukum had decided. She feared the penalty would be death. The royal spring was sacred, she knew, but while discreetly following traditional customs, Shumba often allowed herself to wonder at the fitness of some.

When Ingwa told her the penalty was almost certain to be death or exile, she shuddered. Her empathy for the miserable Bisi was so complete that she grieved as though she herself were forced to leave her children and Bafut. She knew the older woman loved life too much to surrender without a struggle.

"And I don't want you rushing back there to tell her," shouted Ingwa. "She should know by now that if she breaks a law, she must pay for it."

Shumba said nothing. Nevertheless, in the dark of night, she slipped out of the compound again. There was no moon, and even the stars looked cold and lonely. Clouds were looming in the west, and a heavy atmosphere pressed down from the mountains. She slid inaudibly down the path, unaware of the direction her bare feet were taking. She was engrossed in her plan.

When she reached Bisi's place, she noticed a faint light in the large hut. Noiselessly, she went on to Bisi's hut, where she found the culprit weeping quietly, as she had done almost constantly since her imprudent action. Her four children were still kept from her, and this broke her heart and spirit far more than the other punishments.

Shumba told her that the Fon would pronounce sentence the next day. Surely she didn't intend to let herself be killed? Shumba spoke kindly, for she loved this woman as her own sister.

"If I can't have my children, I might as well be dead," moaned the distraught Bisi. "What good is a mother without her children? And now my husband hates me so that I'll never have any more. *Ai-i-ee!*"

Shumba begged her to be quiet and listen to her plan. Because the Fon probably would pronounce a sentence of death, wouldn't it be preferable to go into exile, to flee Bafut in the night? She could make her way to Bamenda or Bali. With the money Shumba had brought with her, she could buy protection and perhaps, because she was still young, strong, and comely, find another husband. The Bali would surely not return her to Bafut; and even in Bamenda she could find help, for a woman who could still work in the fields was a welcome asset.

"But my children? Shall I never see my children again?" wailed Bisi, wanting to flee, but nearly preferring death to life without her babies.

Gently, Shumba put her hand across Bisi's mouth, warning her she'd wake the compound. If she thought the Fon would merely impose the death sentence, she must remember how much he and his wives revered that spring. Without a doubt she would be tortured. She must try to save herself. After more tears and much prodding, Bisi began to realize that her situation was truly hopeless unless she acted. Despite her inactivity of the last month, she was not one to sit and wait for disaster. She decided Shumba was right. Immediately she accepted the money. The women packed a bit of dried meal in a fiber bag. Then they crept out of the compound.

The clouds were scudding high now, ahead of a wind that presaged a storm before morning. The sky was alternately black, gray, and luminous with a faint light from the hills to the south. The two women hastily made their way to the edge of the village, stepping gingerly around the medicine ropes. Tearfully they embraced each other; Shumba begged the older woman to be careful. She peered into the night until she could no longer see the dark figure careening down the path. Then she turned and bolted back to her compound. As she reached the gate, rain began to fall. She worried about Bisi finding some shelter in the night, but she knew that haste was important, because the flight would be discovered early in the morning.

The storm was another bad one, letting loose a cloudburst to the south. In one quarter the roofs of more than a dozen huts were torn off by the violence of the howling winds. Several "toy" huts were destroyed, and this, of course, was an evil omen. Because of the storm the Fon decided to wait and announce Bisi's fate at the weekly market. Her flight was thus not discovered until nearly noon. One of her twins went to the hut with some

This carved wooden mask, which belongs to the Fon, is worn on top of the head, not in front of the face. It is rubbed with charcoal and camwood to bring out the features and to preserve it from termites.

Wood carvings of the Cameroons. Above left—The Fon's mask, of wood covered with cylindrical beads, depicts the forest buffalo, one of the most feared animals. Above right—a beaded stool belonging to the Fon. The seat rests on two leopards, signs of royalty. Below left—royal stool, carved from single tree trunk, with human and animal figures. Below right—a stool of the Fon's, carved with bats' heads.

Life-sized ritual figures are set up in the dance plaza for all special ceremonies. Both are carved of wood and covered with cylindrical beads. The male (left) wears a royal headdress and a blue-and-white Jukun skirt. The female (right) wears the royal cowrie-shell girdle and carries a calabash with life-giving palm wine.

Wearing a beret and a World War I shirt, an old man smokes an intricately carved pipe of the Cameroons. The pipe is made of three materials: the mouthpiece and rod are of brass, the carved stem of wood, and the bowl of pottery.

Houses in the Cameroons are built of raffia palm poles (above), laced into a lattice. Diagonal braces stiffen the walls. The man below thatches a roof, carefully laying elephant grass between the rafters. Both the thatched roof and the outer layer of mud plaster on the walls insulate the houses from the hot tropical sun.

Tax collectors making change. Many of the people of Bafut trade by the old barter system, but they have long been familiar with coins and know how to use them. The coins shown above are the British West African currency used from 1917 until independence, when the franc took over.

Women attend the weekly market to sell their grains and vegetables. Here they trade the produce they have grown for such commodities as salt and English cottons.

Once a week, everyone in Bafut gathers in the marketplace. Even those who have nothing to buy or sell come to find out what's going on. In the midafternoon at each market, Kweyifon, head of the Council of Elders, announces the news.

A young boy sits in a market stall selling salt, which he measures with a British cigarette tin. Salt has to be brought in from the coast, and women work hard to earn "salt money" to pay for it.

In Bafut, where women run the farms, men do most of the handicrafts. Sewing clothes and knitting caps (above) are considered men's work. Basket weaving (below) is one of few crafts done by women.

Achirimbi and some of his wives. It is estimated that he has between seventy-five and eighty, but he never has admitted to more than forty.

Clusters of thatched huts dot the hillsides in the Cameroons. Watered by heavy rainfall, the rugged land is well suited to farming.

Wearing a European dress, Deborah, a favorite wife of the Fon, poses behind the resthouse. In addition to farming her own plot of land, each wife has special duties to perform. Ranking wives wait on guests who visit the royal compound.

Two of the Fon's messengers. Prior to Achirimbi's time, "enchindas" of nine or ten years old were chosen to serve the Fon without pay for a period of about five years. Now, however, Bafut is slowly getting away from the old "enchinda" system. The men below, products of a new era, are hired and paid by the Fon.

Observing the proper way of addressing the Fon, this young man bows slightly and speaks through cupped hands. The Fon reigns as both political and spiritual leader of his kingdom.

*Each spring there is a communal hunt to bring meat to the Fon.
Here, the hunters wait to present their kill.*

A chief export of the Cameroons, palm oil is used for making soap and cosmetics. Above, two workers stir the kernels in a heated pit where the oil will boil off and rise to the top. Below, a man squeezes further oil from the cooked kernels.

This modern family indicates some of the changes that have taken place in Bafut. *All three wear European clothes, and the man wears a watch. In a few years the baby will attend one of the mission or government schools in the village.*

fruit, and when he found her gone, ran to his other "mother" with the news. She immediately told her husband, and the search was on.

When he heard the uproar, Ingwa sternly asked Shumba if she knew what it was; she sat with eyes downcast and said nothing. He rushed out to investigate.

By nightfall it was all over. Bisi's broken body was found near the path to Bamenda, wedged between two gigantic boulders at the bottom of a waterfall. Apparently she had slipped while trying to cross the whirling stream in the darkness. Because of the powerful flow of water from the storm, she had lost the struggle. With no ceremony, they placed her in the ground near the waterfall.

Problem women are no more unusual with the Bafut than they are with any other people. One story they tell concerns that queen mother of long ago who, according to legend, was responsible for bringing her people down from Mbabari to the present site of Bafut.

All went well, goes the story, for several years after the tribe settled at Bafut. But then, as the queen mother grew older, she became like some elderly people, dissatisfied with her lot. She said she had not been given choice land and that it was not close enough to the village. She felt her power was diminishing. When the Fon's wives asked the number-one or number-two wife to make the proper arrangements for visiting their husband at night, the queen mother screamed that she should be consulted. However, this was no longer in her hands, for the Fon at that time had close to fifty wives, all of whom he was expected to impregnate in order to strengthen the tribe. His chief wives were doing an excellent job. But the queen mother realized her grasp on the wives and children, and through them on the Fon himself, was slipping. She couldn't bear to see her authority go unheeded; she became more quarrelsome with each passing year.

As she grew older she grew careless about her person. She no longer had her slaves rub her body carefully with palm oil. If they happened to be gone when she arose early in the morning, she sometimes sluiced herself quickly with water, as did all the royal women and children every morning, but sometimes she neglected it. Often as not she berated her slaves spitefully, for no reason at all.

The wives and sisters of the king were aware the queen mother was stirring up trouble among them, playing the older wives against the younger, the women from one lineage against those of another. They were powerless to stop her. She had always enjoyed her palm wine, but now she drank so much she was inebriated a great deal of the time.

All of this the people understood, although they disliked it. But then they had two crop failures in succession, and for no apparent reason, sickness befell the village. There must be a witch in their midst, the people murmured.

One day, as the Council of Elders was discussing an important case with the Fon, the queen mother ran into his compound, wild-eyed and raving. She screamed that one of the Fon's younger wives had stolen a gourd of wine from her hut, and she wanted the girl put to death immediately.

The Fon commanded her to hold her tongue, to wait with her complaints until the proper time for such things. But nothing would silence the old virago. Her face gleamed with sweat as she berated, shouted, cajoled, and cried. Little flecks of spittle ran down her chin. The elders sat aghast. Finally, some of the older women came in and dragged her out of the yard, back to her own hut.

Watching this spectacle, in front of the Fon himself, the elders decided the time had come to do something drastic. They asked the Fon's permission to consult the diviner. They were convinced they had a witch on their hands. The Fon was not so sure, but he could not hold out against them. He agreed they should go to the diviner. He alone could determine whether or not she was a witch and what could be done about it.

Taking with them a goat, some palm wine, and a bag of valuable beads, the two most important elders went to the diviner the next day. As they approached his mud hut, the old man walked out to greet them. He had already guessed why they were there, for news of the queen mother's behavior had traveled through the entire village. He was a slight man with a nose too large for his face. Around his middle was a narrow dirty piece of bark cloth. He invited them to sit down, and his assistant brought them palm wine.

After the proper interval of talking desultorily about nothing and drinking copious quantities of wine, Kweyifon disclosed their predicament. Was the Fon's mother the cause of the sickness and crop failures?

At this the diviner went into his hut. He emerged carrying a fiber bag, black with the smoke of many fires. With great deliberation he took from it two little stones, two pieces of pitch, a red feather, a human jawbone, a small piece of quartz, and a small section of gourd. Carefully, he arranged these on the ground in the prescribed circular position. The quartz was the symbol of the king; it had to be present in order to observe what was about to happen. After placing seven cowrie shells in the center, the diviner was ready to begin.

Kweyifon repeated his question: Was the queen mother the cause of the crop failure and the sickness in Bafut? The diviner picked up the cowries in his fist and held them a moment to Kweyifon's forehead. The shells were then tossed down amid the other sacred objects, and as they came to rest the diviner was able to read them. He said nothing, but picked them up and laid them aside. He picked up the red feather, and after holding it to Kweyifon's forehead, let it flutter to the ground in the center of the ring. He noted the direction it faced and whether it stopped closer to the stones or near the jawbone. Lastly, he picked up the piece of gourd and lightly touched it to Kweyifon's forehead. As it was cast into the center of the ring, he looked up at the two elders with a sad expression.

The diviner spoke at last. The signs indicated the queen mother had used her magic to bring sickness to the village. It was almost certain, too, that she had caused the crop failure, although this was not so strongly indicated.

Kweyifon puffed silently on his pipe for a while and then asked the diviner what course of action they should take. As he spoke, the second elder handed over a particularly beautiful bead, large and ellipsoid, with gleaming blue, white, and yellow designs. The diviner accepted it with a deferential nod and picked up the human mandible. He cast this into the circle and, as it fell, shuddered slightly. He looked into the faces of the two men. If they wanted to rid the village of sickness and have a successful crop, he said, they must eliminate the queen mother.

When the two elders reached the royal compound that evening, the entire council had been assembled. Palm wine was being passed by the enchindas. When the Fon entered, the men stood up, clapped three times, bowed to him, and greeted him in low voices through cupped hands. As he sat on his carved stool, they sank to the ground and waited for Kweyifon to make his report. The Fon asked a few of the men about affairs in various quarters of the village. An important question was never dealt with immediately, but rather approached as one would a wounded animal—first from one side, then from the other, to be sure there was no escape.

Finally, the Fon turned to Kweyifon and asked him if he had seen the diviner. The old man spoke carefully, for this was going to be a painful report. The diviner had read the signs with discretion and reached the conclusion that the queen mother was not only the cause of the sickness of the village but was spreading her evil by inducing the crop failures. Moreover, unless the village was cleansed of her presence, things could grow worse.

At this the Council of Elders broke into loud talking and rough gesticulation. The Fon was silent. All were trying to insinuate their ideas of the best way to release the people from this monster. The Fon asked each man to explain his method. Some wanted banishment, some advocated imprisonment in a small cage placed in a stream, some thought the sassywood ordeal would prove effective, and one suggested that she be tied to an anthill, which would mean slow and painful death. Finally, Kweyifon stood up once more.

"We will not be free of this evil until the queen mother is dead," he said. "Let us bury her alive."

A shout of approval went up from all twelve men.

The rest of the night the men talked of their plans for saving the village. It must be done in the strictest secrecy, for the queen mother had her spies. Some men were given the task of selecting the place of murder; some were to spread stories through the entire Bafut area about the homage to be paid her, for they had decided that to allay her suspicions they would build a new throne and offer her extravagant gifts as a reward for the role she had played in finding the Bafut site.

During the next week, at night and in deepest secrecy, a huge pit was prepared. It was twelve feet deep, three feet wide, and six feet long, similar to the traps they fashioned to ambush leopards. The pit was skillfully concealed with light branches, soft earth, and leaves. On the platform stood a handsome carved chair and next to it a small table with palm wine in a carved drinking cup. After a few days, some of the councilors went to the queen mother, and with stories of the homage they were prepared to pay her, lured her to the pitfall. A tremendous crowd, shouting and pushing, was gathered to watch this momentous event.

Ecstatic with the idea that she had won over her enemies and elated with her new throne, the queen mother walked quickly to the chair and sat down. The platform collapsed, hurling her to the bottom of the pit. Immediately, the men rushed up to cover her with dirt. In spite of her screams and imprecations, the crowd roared its approval.

After the hole was completely filled in, two fig trees were planted over her grave, trees that are now very tall and still grow in the small market square not far from the royal compound. These are sacred trees and must never be cut down. The place was called "The Spot of a God," for after this the queen mother was revered as such. Following her ignominious burial they held a funeral service for her, killing many goats and declaring that there would be no more unusual deaths in Bafut.

Under the Tribal Shield

Although Bafut breathed more easily after Bisi's tragedy, for more than a month the medicine ropes remained on the paths and the tiny "toy" huts were reerected. No more dreadful storms occurred the rest of the year. There were only the usual rains, heavy in the afternoons and early evenings, followed by clear skies again for a few hours. The crops appeared to be maturing well, and the people looked forward to a full harvest.

Then, on the heels of the rainy season, without warning, came disaster: smallpox. Before the people could gather their medicines together, half the tribe was stricken. Two of Ingwa's wives and some of his children were taken sick. Shumba begged her husband to flee before he too became ill. The Fon fled with Ingwa, Muma, and others to Bande, leaving Kweyifon and a few elders to help the medicine society give relief to the sick and bury the dead. Shumba chose to remain and help with the nursing. When the British administration finally learned of the epidemic, they sent a team of medical officers, but for a good part of the population it was too late.

Before the fever spent itself, many of Ingwa's family and friends lay dead. Ashoh, his mother, was one of the first to die. Bisi's husband and one of her twins, old Shu, the teacher's father —all dead! Two of Ingwa's younger sons were stricken and one died. The other lived through the frightful illness but remained horribly disfigured. Nearly everyone he knew was touched by the epidemic; many of the survivors carried pockmarks for the rest of their lives.

Several owls, birds of evil omen, had hovered for weeks in the vicinity. In spite of their presence, everyone blamed Bisi for the pestilence. Shumba could weep only in her heart, for no one knew she had aided Bisi in her flight. If Ingwa suspected, he never confronted her with it. With his usual perception he may have decided she had paid for her folly by her valiant nursing during the epidemic.

Slowly Bafut returned to normal. Many younger men had lost their fathers in the epidemic; Fontwi, Ingwa's ugly little cousin, was one of them. He was now asked to return to his old home, to assume his father's name and prestige as the new compound head. Because his father, Tahla, had been a quarterhead and a member of the Bukum, the king himself would bestow the new name on Fontwi. It was not necessarily the oldest son who received this legacy, but rather one whom the father had secretly chosen and whose identity had been imparted only to the Fon and a few close friends and relatives. Fontwi's sagacity in business, his perceptiveness, and his agreeable personality had long been recognized by old Tahla.

The ceremony, which was held in the royal compound, was not as lavish as those in happier days. The people were still recovering from the effects of the tragic smallpox epidemic. Accompanied by his wives and children, all carrying tribute to the Fon, Fontwi was escorted by his father's oldest brother. The rest of the family followed. With the weight of his new responsibilities, Fontwi now bore himself with an unaccustomed dignity. He heard his uncle give a short speech and then present him to the Fon as the new head of the compound. Rubbing a bit of powdered camwood on Fontwi's head, the Fon called him Tahla; he would henceforth be the head and father of his lineage. In Bafut a lineage included all those persons who could trace their ancestry to one male progenitor. The new Tahla knelt before the king, and cupping his hands drank the palm wine as Aboumbi poured it out of the beaker. By this gesture he indicated his allegiance to the king and his willingness to assume the name and the responsibilities incumbent upon the head of the lineage.

The Fon informed the crowd that long before old Tahla died, he had secretly indicated which son he wished to carry his name and his obligations. Pulling Tahla to his feet, the Fon told him to return to his father's home. His father's wives would become Tahla's wives, and he must care for all of them to the end of their days. He now inherited his father's property, his trees, his children, and his liabilities. His brothers would call him "Father," for he was now the father of the lineage. If he did justice to the name of Tahla, he would glorify the memory of his dead father, a worthy and illustrious man.

Tahla whispered his thanks to the Fon. Then, at the head of the procession, he led his family to their new quarters, where they celebrated with a short feast. Everyone made obeisance to him as the new head of the lineage. His wives now numbered fifteen. He told them he would take full responsibility for all of them in memory of his dead father; but if any of them could no longer care for their farms, they were free to live with any married children, if they so wished. Fortunately, three of the oldest women had married daughters who invited them to move in. His old compound, with its trees, kitchen gardens, huts, and storage areas, which had formerly housed his three wives and their children, Tahla presented to one of his younger brothers.

As the head of the lineage now, Tahla was expected to give presents to his numerous relatives and to help in numerous ways all male members of the family. As the tribe was the protective shield under which each family could seek refuge in time of need, so the lineage served as a bulwark to each individual. It protected him from danger, bolstered his sagging spirits, afforded him a good start in the secret societies. It provided aid and comfort when he was sick. A lineage member—or a tribal member, for that matter—as long as he observed the tribal laws, need never feel alone, unavowed, or abandoned. He knew exactly what was expected of him, and if he failed, social discipline was usually enough to set him back on the tribal path. Tahla was an exemplary Bafut man, and he ruled his lineage with strength and firmness.

A few years later, when he had finished paying the requisite fees, Tahla attained full membership in the Bukum. He had served the Fon as an enchinda for three years only, for his service had been interrupted when he was wounded in a tribal skirmish. The young man had matured commendably, however, and proved his worth during the German battles. His close association with Ingwa was a boon to them both. Tahla served as a liaison man between the royal compound and the several outlying quarters near his home. His wisdom and subtle skill in dealing with people made him a valuable member of the Bukum. His many business ventures continued to bring wealth and prestige to the tribe.

One afternoon, Chunga saw one of Ingwa's younger sons approaching him on the village path. The youth carried a small fiber hood and an empty calabash. Chunga asked why he was in such a hurry. The boy replied that he was taking his juju mask and drum to his uncle Neba's compound. He and his friends planned to practice funeral songs and dances. This was another approach used by the boys to learn the songs and dances of their elders. Each quarter had a club of around thirty boys. These small juju societies were made up primarily of the children of commoners, but Ingwa's young son had talked his way into this one. Because of his admirable singing voice, they had accepted him. The calabash served as the drum, because the children could not afford a real one. The boy stored it in his mother's hut. Besides dancing and singing for fun, they occasionally pranced through the village, begging tiny gifts. If a member or the mother of a member died, the children went in their group to sing and dance.

With a friendly grin, Chunga told the boy that one of his little girls, nearly three, cried too much. He asked his nephew to come to his compound soon and frighten her with his juju hood. The boy laughed and promised to come.

When Chunga reached his enclosure, he found Ingwa, Kimi, and Tahla waiting for him. By their faces he knew it was a solemn visit. In his low, pleasant voice he greeted them. Had his wives brought them wine? The men nodded; his wives had done their duty.

A few weeks before, Kimi's youngest wife had thought she saw an owl in their compound. Everyone knew that an owl was one of the most evil omens. She was frantic, and when she reported it to Kimi, he tried to allay her fears. But yesterday their little boy had become gravely ill. It was necessary to consult a diviner. Tahla insisted that he go to the one in his quarter, whereas Ingwa thought the old diviner near the market was better. Kimi wanted Chunga's advice. Chunga pondered, then came out in favor of Ingwa's diviner.

This was a serious affair. The little boy was choked up with his illness and could scarcely breathe. When the four men went to the diviner near the market, he told them that apparently one of Kimi's old, deceased uncles was not satisfied with the way an old injustice had been settled. He kept "coming out of his grave" to bring sickness to Kimi's family.

The following day, the diviner led the four men and Kimi's wives and sons to the compound where the old uncle was buried. Here, behind the main hut, he cleaned off the grave, exposing the bamboo pipe that led down to the dead man's mouth. Kimi had brought a cock and a hen as well as a large calabash of palm wine. The diviner killed the fowls and poured their blood into the small hole. He covered it up and built a fire over the grave. The fowls were roasted, salted, and cut into pieces.

Kimi was the senior man in his compound, so it was he who talked to his dead ancestor. He said they had come to offer food and wine, so he would forgive any injury or injustice done to him while he was still alive. Kimi poured a little palm wine over the spot where the blood had been spilled. If this spirit was the one bringing the sickness, Kimi begged him to stop. After this plea, the diviner, Kimi, his wives and children, Chunga, Tahla, and Ingwa sat down. They consumed the chickens and drank the wine. They conversed in low voices for a while. Then they went home. The sick boy's mother met Kimi at the gate, her face drawn with worry. She asked her husband what had happened.

As best he could, Kimi soothed her. They would have to wait a few days. If the sickness was not arrested, if the old uncle still "came out of his grave," it would be necessary to dig up the skeleton and burn his bones. This would completely destroy the spirit of the dead man and make him incapable of further action.

But the next morning, when Kimi went to his wife's hut to inquire about the boy, he was met at the door by a calm and tranquil mother. Her son was better; the fever was gone, and he breathed more easily. The old uncle had accepted the offerings.

The child lay on a fiber mat near the fire. Two of Kimi's wives were there, helping the mother tend her sick child. In his softest voice, Kimi talked to the boy, stroking the little shoulders and forehead with tender fingers. One of the wives came forward with a small calabash of hot broth and a tiny piece of meat. Kimi took the meat, chewed it until it was tender, and placed it in the boy's mouth. Slowly he fed the broth to the child until the bowl was empty. The mother murmured that it was the first food the child had eaten since the fever started. Gratefully she assured Kimi their son would praise him as long as he lived.

Just then, Kimi noticed a little frog in the corner of the hut, a sacred frog that would bring good luck. He picked it up, and after rubbing a bit of powdered camwood along its back, carried it to the door and gently placed it on the ground. This was a good omen. As their son drifted into the sleep which would assure his return to health, the parents smiled at each other.

The King Is Dead,
Long Live the King

The years had been kind to Ingwa. In the spring of 1932 he was about forty-eight years old. He was in good health, with over a dozen wives, numerous children, and more wealth than he really needed. His tremendous prestige among his fellow tribesmen was recognized by the British administrators in Bamenda. He was still slender, still lithe and active, a good hunter and fighter, and a creditable drummer and dancer. He was wily and arrogant when it served his purpose, but he was also the model of justice, tenderness, and compassion with his favorite wives and children.

The spring rains were over and had settled, finally, into the long rainy season. Aboumbi developed an illness that did not respond to any Bafut treatment. He was old, true, but his mind had lost none of its alertness. He insisted upon regular consultations with his Council of Elders and the Bukum. Many of his dissident sons had ceased their agitation to massacre a successor, for they realized that the decision had been made long ago; there was nothing they could now do. Most of the men had adjusted to the situation. They pursued their daily business without fretting over an heir. Their chief concern now was the state of the Fon's health.

But as his illness became more apparent, some of them began, again, to mutter about his successor. Muma, old Kweyifon, and several of the council were in daily attendance at the palace. Aboumbi lay in the Achum, his stately hut in the center of the royal compound. A fire burned constantly, for the rains brought a chill to the air that made the old king's suffering even more intense. Most of the wives were barred from the Achum; only the two oldest were allowed to slip in at night to see him and talk quietly with him. They assured the others that he was still alive.

At the beginning of August, Ingwa and several of his wives and children returned late one afternoon from the second die-cry of one of Kimi's relatives. It had been a day-long ceremony. Gifts of food, cotton cloth, and palm wine were given the deceased's brothers and uncles. Huge amounts of gunpowder had been shot off out of respect to the dead man's spirit. Nearly all of Ingwa's favorite friends were there to drum and dance: Chunga, Ndi, and Tahla, who was now an important man in the Bukum. During a lull in the ceremonies, they talked about the sick king, his chances for survival through the rains, and who his successor might be. No doubt, each son secretly hoped he had been chosen, but they no longer joked about it as they had in the old days. When they returned to the village and their own homes, the rain began again, monotonous in its regularity, filling earth and sky with a sodden veil.

In their compound, Shumba and Mankana directed their daughters to stir up the fire in their father's hut, for Ingwa would sit smoking a while before he retired. His two oldest wives often sat with him, but tonight all were uncommonly tired. Soon after dark the compound was silent, save for the dripping of water off the trees into innumerable puddles. Then the rain halted, and the frogs and night birds began their incessant songs.

Suddenly, Ingwa was roused from a deep sleep by a low voice at his elbow. It was one of Kweyifon's enchindas, telling him to come immediately to the royal compound; he was warned to speak to no one on the way. Hurriedly, the prince slipped on a Cameroons gown and placed his Cameroons cap on the back of his shaved head. He scorned the slippers he had lately begun to wear, for in the dark night he knew he would be more surefooted in his bare feet.

Years before his illness—no one ever knew when their decision had been made—the king, Kweyifon, and three of the Council of Elders had discussed which son should be chosen as heir. The prime requisite was that the candidate have been conceived on a leopard skin. In addition, he must be brave, slow to anger, prudent, sagacious. He must possess the ability to lead the people through the many vicissitudes that were constantly befalling them.

The manner in which Ingwa fought against the Germans had

made a deep impression on several of the elders, as had his aptitude for handling people, both European and African. His kindness and dignity, his patience and resourcefulness, his wide knowledge of Bafut traditions, together with his sense of propriety and his famous sense of humor, were all qualities important in a chieftain.

Chunga, on the other hand, was thought to have a deeper understanding of the white man, because he had worked for a while with the Germans and later with the British in Bamenda. In spite of his quick temper, he was considered to have the sobriety a chief could use to advantage. Both young men had benefited from their schooling in the German mission school. Together with several other brothers, particularly Ndi and Neba, they were well qualified as candidates for the Fon's stool—that is, the throne or the position itself.

Finally, the choice was narrowed to Ingwa and Chunga. Both men had over a dozen wives, who had given them fine children; they were outstanding in the tribe for their industry, bravery, and knowledge of ritual; and both possessed the courtliness so appreciated by the Bafut. Ingwa's lusty sense of humor merely proved he was a good man.

It was a lengthy discussion, and the elders took months to work out the pros and cons. When the final decision was reached, Ingwa was the chosen son. Because only the Fon and the four elders knew the choice, they had ample opportunity to observe the candidate, unaware of his future role, in his daily activities, his duties at court, his relations with his brothers and other relatives, his behavior toward the Council of Elders, and his handling of Native Authority matters.

Ingwa and his escort walked noiselessly toward the palace, exchanging not a word. Perhaps he guessed why he had been summoned, but he had been imbued at an early age with the spirit of absolute obedience; he never questioned his being roused in the middle of the night. All was quiet as they entered the majestic Achum. Only the king's oldest wife had been told of this latest illness; she sat outside the door of the great house sobbing silently. Her thin breasts were pressed tightly to her body with tired hands, her grizzled head caught the light from the perpetual fire burning in the inner room. Ingwa knew she wondered why he was there. Suddenly, it crossed his mind that his father must be very ill indeed.

As he passed through the double walls of this house that always gave him a sense of tranquility, the prince could see the elders, seated near the fire, smoking calmly. Some held wine cups in their hands. One of them asked the enchinda if they had been observed, but the man assured him they had hurried along the path with all discretion.

Ingwa was motioned to a fiber mat. He wondered where his father was, and shuddered to think why no one mentioned him. Someone poured a little palm wine into a cup and handed it to him. He walked over to the ancestor stone, poured a small libation on it, then drank slowly, aware that every movement was being watched by these taciturn men.

Kweyifon came out of the inner room. He nodded to Ingwa and, in a low voice, announced that the Fon was not well. Long ago, he continued, while the Fon was still in good health, he had chosen Ingwa and Chunga to be the candidates for his stool.

With his blood pounding in his ear, Ingwa tried to keep his voice even. If Chunga was the chosen one, he told them, he would do his best as his right hand.

Kweyifon looked at him for a long, long moment.

"Chunga was not chosen," he said. "The Fon wished you to be his successor. We have concurred with him in this, for we believe you will be a wise and strong leader."

Ingwa sat so still that one of the men next to him thought he had not heard. Then he rose to his feet and asked to see his father.

Kweyifon told him they did not know how long the Fon would live. He had asked that Ingwa be brought to him now so he could pass on his divine power. Ingwa was led into the inner room.

On a dais covered with a leopard skin lay the sick Fon, a Jukun cloth thrown over his middle. His eyes were open, gazing up at the fiber ceiling, but his face looked gray, with the skin pulled tightly over the nose and cheekbones. His wife had slipped in while the men were talking; now she arose, and with a pitiful gesture of surrender, shuffled out of the room. She had been married to the Fon for an unmeasured number of years. She had hoped that one of her sons might be his heir, but she knew now it was not to be.

Ingwa knelt beside his father as Kweyifon helped the old king to a sitting position. Aboumbi focused his tired eyes on his son. With difficulty, he whispered that he had not long to live; soon the old men would bury him in this Achum, and his soul would go to live with the other chiefs in the sacred lake. He sank back a little, each sentence a great effort. The perspiration stood out on his forehead, yet his mouth was dry. Someone held a cup to his lips, and he drank a little wine.

"You, of all my sons, I wish to be my successor. I knew a long time ago that you would be a great man. You must be very wise, my son, for there will be troubled times. You must not fail me; you must listen to the voices of your ancestors!"

Suddenly the Fon sat erect and Ingwa bent forward. Pursing his mouth slightly, the old man spat full upon the chest of the newly appointed heir.

"To you, Achirimbi, I pass on my divinity!" he murmured. And with these words the Fon sank back on his bed, breathing with difficulty. Ingwa shivered, trembling slightly. He felt a stabbing in his breast as the spittle ran slowly down his gown. Then one of the elders took Ingwa by the elbow and raised him to his feet. Slowly they moved backward from the chamber. When they reached the outer room, Kweyifon instructed the prince to return to his home with the same escort and to say nothing of what had transpired that night. Each night he would return, to learn certain precepts and receive further necessary training so he would be ready to assume the chieftainship when the Fon died. He was warned again to tell no one; if his brothers knew what had happened, his life would, again, be in jeopardy.

"Sleep well, Achirimbi!"

Kweyifon smiled slightly as he used the new name, but Ingwa knew that he would not be Fon or formally receive his new name until his father died.

For weeks the old king lay ill in the Achum. He grew neither worse nor better. The people commiserated; they feasted, they danced, they sang their ritual songs far into the night, but nothing helped. Finally, when they sensed that the Fon would not improve, everyone wondered aloud about the identity of his successor.

Once or twice Ingwa thought he saw Shumba gazing at him in a quizzical manner, but she said nothing. Fond as they were of each other, it was not for her to speak of such matters to her husband. Sometimes she heard him slip out of the compound at night, but she held her counsel.

A few weeks later Ingwa heard Kweyifon's voice outside his door. He sent Shumba back to her own hut, telling her not to say anything of his absence. Then he put on a clean robe, a pair of sandals, and his Cameroons cap and took his walking stick. Kweyifon met him at the gate, and as they walked to the Achum, he noticed that the royal compound was quiet, with just an undercurrent of whispering from the women's huts. No children were to be seen. Muma stood at the top of the basalt steps. As Ingwa mounted them, his uncle nodded.

The king was dead.

In the first room there was diligent activity; several enchindas were busy digging a large hole to one side of the stones where the fire burned. The Fon had died around sunset. Already one of the enchindas had started for Bamenda with a rope of the sacred grass that grew around the base of the ritual stone in the plaza. It was a message to the District Officer saying that the Fon was dead. The people would not be informed until the day after tomorrow, the day of the week set aside to worship the dead Fon. Until then, Achirimbi must be protected. He would have to stay in the compound under close guard. Alone, he stepped into the inner room to salute his father for the last time.

Aboumbi, "He Who Rules the World," was wrapped in a white cotton cloth; near his head lay a round, white stone. Flat and shining from the tumbling waters of Menchem Falls, this was the stone that had been touched to the Fon's mouth as he gasped his last breath. Into it, it was thought, went a part of Aboumbi's soul. This ancestor stone would be placed just inside the door of the Achum as the new recipient of future libations. It is possible that formerly it would have been the skull of an ancestor, but during tribal wars, no doubt, it was too difficult to carry the heads of their dead when they were forced to flee. These white, water-washed stones were excellent substitutes.

For nearly an hour Ingwa sat alone, talking to his dead father. He promised he would strive to be as good a ruler as Aboumbi had been; he vowed he would consult his father in times of sickness and stress; he prayed that his father would render support for the future. When he left the room, he was consoled and comforted.

The body of the dead Fon was then borne to the main room, where the grave had been finished. The men had dug an opening large enough to hold the sacred stool, deep enough—about six feet—so the old king could be placed in a sitting position. The dirt walls were shored up with bamboo poles. When they had seated the corpse, they placed a long, upright tube of bamboo in his mouth and next to him his favorite bronze pipe and carved drinking cup. He was gorgeously arrayed in the finest robes. In the old days, several wives and slaves would have been buried with the dead monarch, but this custom had now ceased. Finally, the hollow shaft was closed off and dirt thrown over it, leaving the bamboo tube protruding a bit above the ground. Down this conduit libations would be poured on holy days and whenever his intercession was needed. The tube was covered with several stones. The sacred ancestor stone was placed near the door. The old stone would later be deposited at the sacred lake.

All that night and the next day, Ingwa remained in the Achum. Food and palm wine were brought in, and the Council of Elders conversed in low tones. When some left for other parts of the compound, others stayed on watch while Ingwa retired to the inner room to rest. None of the wives were permitted to enter the Achum. They had not been told of the Fon's death, but several of them had seen Ingwa, and they surmised the reason for his presence.

Before dawn on the second day, Ingwa fired a shot, the signal of the Fon's death. In the huge square the big drum began to sing its doleful message. The news spread quickly. So sinister and sad a rhythm could only mean that the Fon was dead.

When they heard the shot and the drumming, the royal wives burst into anguished weeping. Then, with much sobbing, they helped each other prepare for mourning. The older women gave instructions to those whose knowledge of the proper ritual was only hearsay, for this funeral ceremony for a divine king was far more formidable than any held for a mortal man. When the wives were ready to file out into the plaza, their heads had been shaved clean; their badges of royalty, the cowrie bracelets and girdles, had been removed; their bodies were completely covered with ashes. Their tiny babies had been given to relatives to hold; the older children tagged along behind. Some mothers had their faces painted with red camwood, for they were the mothers of twins. All of them were completely naked, save for their "robes" of ashes.

Before the dawn broke, Bafut women, wearing only short fiber skirts of dried plantain leaves, began arriving at the square. Their faces and bodies had been liberally smeared with ashes. They brought offerings of food, which they placed on a great pile in the center of the square; during the day, anyone who wished could help himself to the food. The loud wails of the townswomen soon mingled with those of the wives, sisters, and daughters of the Fon, all grieving together. Sometimes their weeping was soft and subdued; then, rising on the morning air, their shrieks and lamentations echoed into the mountains and came singing back. As one wife after another sank exhausted to the ground, to lie in misery while gathering strength for more grieving, the sisters and relatives stood close at hand, compassionate and forbearing.

Bafut tribesmen from the surrounding area began to stream into the village. As the gloomy daylight slowly warmed the vast square, a semblance of organization became apparent. Members of the secret societies had gone up into the hills to fire their dane guns so that the entire countryside would be aware of their mourning. Returning to the square, they ran around the field, prancing in the traditional military cadence, firing their guns, saluting each other, saluting important men, saluting the dead king. Subchieftains and their retinues from Wum, Bande, and Babanki began to arrive; representatives of the Fons at Kom and Banso arrived during the next few days.

All the secret societies were there, some in feathered cloaks and knit hoods, some with magnificent feathered headdresses. One society wore, atop their heads, black wooden masks, a few in the form of human faces, others representing the bush cow. As they danced by, they flailed their spears at anyone who stood near. Certain military members wore their German sabers and blew German bugles, items of war they still possessed from 1916 and 1917, when they fought with their old conquerors against the British. The jesters rustled past, dressed in long skirts of dried plantain leaves. With bizarre white motifs painted on their faces they groveled in the dust, spears of bamboo thrust into their mouths. The crowd loved it; this was the comedy relief, the release of tension that all mourning must have, the ebb and flow of laughter with the tears.

By early afternoon, the crowd began to thin out a little. Many of them, exhausted with the noise and weeping, slowly returned to their homes. In the center of the square, the huge pile of food had disappeared, and the wretched widows, moaning piteously, were sitting near a makeshift altar, a fiber square, held together with bamboo fronds. In its center was one lone banana stalk. The sons of the Fon had set this up as the symbol of their dead father. It was carefully protected by armed guards, stalwart fellows who glared menacingly at anyone who came too close. Above it flew the red and white flag of Aboumbi. Day and night this symbol was closely guarded, for whoever stole that would have stolen the person of the chief.

Soon after dark the village was calm, but for an occasional drumming in a few of the compounds. The people whispered together, then drifted off to sleep. The talk was mostly of the new chief. Who would it be? In the huge multitude that gathered in the square, Ingwa had not been missed. Only his wives and his closest associates, Chunga, Tahla, and Ndi, realized he was gone. But they said nothing.

Five days the entire Bafut area mourned for their dead king. Nearly twenty thousand people milled in and out of the village. Five days the mountains echoed with their moaning, singing, and wailing, with their drumming and their shooting. Each day people brought food to pile in the center of the square near the symbolic altar; by noon it had disappeared. Each day gifts of goat, antelope, leopard skins, ivory, guns, ammunition, palm wine, and palm oil were brought to the royal compound—gifts from neighboring tribes, gifts in memory of Aboumbi, gifts to honor the new king not yet named.

On the sixth day the ceremonies began as usual, but as morning wore on, the royal compound began to stir with activity. The daughters of the dead Fon came out with wands of horsetail, the handles intertwined with finely beaded designs. They waved them rhythmically to and fro as they danced sedately in a single line around the square. At the head of their procession, the two eldest held high, like standards, two lustrous leopard skins.

After them, the Fon's sisters, in a long, thin trail, went round and round the field. Each one carried something: long-necked calabashes heavily embellished with beads; European trade articles of glass, tall, shapely vases, cut-glass pitchers, or English portrait mugs. Delicately, they minced once around the square, their skirts of dried leaves swaying and swishing with their dancing motions. Then they disappeared behind the fiber gate.

About noon, the door in the compound wall opened. The military society began to clear a path through the crowd, which had suddenly quieted to a hum. The Bukum filed through the door, followed by three juju men in their hooded costumes. Kweyifon was next, announced by the clinking sound of his spear. His face was covered by a fiber net, and he wore a special necklace of plaited fiber made from sacred grass, which grew at the base of the ritual stone in the dance plaza.

Close behind him was the new chief, Achirimbi II. He was naked, save for a white loincloth folded about his hips. In his right hand he carried the Cameroons staff, with three small red feathers sprouting from the top—the touraco feathers awarded for killing a bush cow, a leopard, or a man. He strode out into the crowd, fearlessly showing the Bafut tribe that he was their new Fon.

Suddenly, the two Bukum who were bringing up the rear of the procession stopped in their tracks. Achirimbi turned and began to run back toward the palace. The Council of Elders tried to protect him as he ran. But the people had armed themselves with small stones and clods of earth, and now they began throwing these at the new chief. Everyone tried to assure himself that his stone actually touched Achirimbi. This symbolic gesture indicated that the people, who were mortal, had just elevated one of their own number to a position of immortality. From this day on, he could not be touched by anyone. He was thenceforth a divine king, with powers of life and death over his twenty thousand subjects. This was their last chance to touch him while he was yet mortal. He was not hurt in the stoning; the few welts raised by flying pebbles would soon heal.

As he was led to his father's house, the home he would never leave again, Achirimbi noted that one of the enchindas was leading Shumba, Mankana, and his other wives and their children through the public gate into the yard where the younger women lived. As he went into the Achum to prepare for the evening of dancing and receptions for visitors, a great joy welled up inside him.

Out in the vast plaza, people were dispersing. They went down to the stream to wash away their signs of mourning and returned to their homes for fresh clothing. The men put on their finest robes and the women their loveliest beaded girdles, for in the evening the entire tribe would return to dance and chant their praises of the new king.

Only the widows and their children were left in the plaza, sitting desolately around the symbolic emblem of the old chief. They didn't know what their fate would be, although they automatically became the wives and wards of Achirimbi. For a while they simply sagged on the ground, too exhausted to move back into their homes. At last, the sisters of the old Fon came out. With the help of some of the older children, they persuaded the widows to return to their huts. Most of them fell into a deep, dull sleep; the others slowly washed off the mourning signs and then tried to take up their household tasks. But they were too numb; one by one they slipped into their huts to rest. Later that night they would dance; now they slept as though drugged.

After dark the royal yards began to fill with visiting dignitaries and Bafut tribesmen. One after another, in a long line, Achirimbi's brothers, his sons, the important members of the Bukum, and lastly his wives, filed past the carved stool under the colossal fig tree. Achirimbi II sat with his feet on an ivory tusk. He wore a gorgeous velvet robe of red, black, and yellow, so encrusted with embroidery that it glittered in the firelight. On the back of his head was a tight fiber cap to which were fastened long elephant-tail bristles that somewhat shielded his face. These shot out from his head like rays and gave him an awesome appearance. His stool was partially covered with a leopard skin, and blue-and-white Jukan cloths were draped behind him. Beaded slippers covered his feet. In his left hand he carried the royal fly whisk. Old Muma was proud of him.

Soberly the new Fon poured endless quantities of palm wine directly from the horn cup into the hands of his subjects, who all vowed their allegiance by kneeling before him and drinking his wine. The next day he would meet with the Bukum. He would announce whom he had selected to serve in the places of honor at his right and at his left. The next day, he would choose a number-one wife to superintend the affairs of his wives and children. The next day he would pick up the reins of the kingdom and begin a new regime.

Tonight, he was a divine king dispensing life-giving wine to his people, thereby assuring them that the life blood of the Bafut tribe would go on forever.

Achirimbi II, He Who Lives Eternally, had assumed his throne.

In the Spirit of His Ancestors

With all the retainers, servants, enchindas, wives, and other personnel of the royal court going about their appointed tasks, life again assumed a normal pattern after the "raising up" of Achirimbi to his father's stool. He assured all his father's wives that they need have no concern for their future. Because some were old and had no families to whom they could turn, this was welcome security. The younger women, royal still, became Achirimbi's own wives in fact as well as by ceremony. The wives he brought with him were regal now, but aside from this change in status, their lives were visibly not much altered. In fact, now that they were forced to share their royal husband with fifty or more other women, not a few longed for the good old days, when they had more opportunities for intimacy with Ingwa.

Shumba and Mankana, still his most favored and trusted wives, were elevated to the ranking positions. This high status automatically earned them the envy of every other wife and the outright enmity of some. But Achirimbi was fond of these two, and he knew they were intelligent, impartial, and forthright. He was certain they would soon earn the respect of the entire court.

Following the daily routine of his father, Achirimbi arose about sunup (roughly about six o'clock) each morning. A colorful gown and woven cap were laid out for him by Shumba or Mankana. Sometimes he hid his dark features beneath a rough, broad-brimmed hat. Once in a while he slipped his feet into sandals, shoes, or beaded slippers, but more often he went barefoot. When he was dressed he commenced his tour of inspection, usually accompanied by one of the more important wives and one or two enchindas.

The compound had long been divided into a yard for older women and one for those with small children.

Achirimbi, who remembered the neatness he had learned from the Germans, couldn't abide slovenliness. His new wives soon learned to keep their yards in order. Negligence moved him to sudden anger, and he would order fines levied on those wives who were lax in their housekeeping. Sometimes, good housekeeping involved unusual problems. Once a green mamba, a deadly poisonous snake, slithered across the yard. One of the older wives slashed it in two with her bush knife, but left it lying on the ground. The Fon was furious with this untidiness, and ordered the carcass removed at once; nothing must mar the clean expanse of the enclosure. All the women, often assisted by the enchindas, cooperated in carrying out the work of tidying up after a heavy rain or sweeping the extensive courtyards after a celebration.

When Achirimbi returned from his morning tour of inspection, some of his older sons might be waiting with their problems. If a few of the council came in, he chatted with them. Then he would give his attention to the court messengers who had been sifting the supplications or complaints of the townspeople. If a case was serious, a day would be set for the hearing. Possibly it would be referred to the Native Authority Court.

After these discussions, which were usually held in the "yard for the chief's women," Achirimbi returned to the Achum, where a bath would have been prepared. At this time he was shaved by one of his ranking wives. Because of his sparse beard, this was done only every third or fourth day.

A junior wife became a ranking one by imploring the Fon for the privilege; she accompanied her request with a goat or a few fowl and a gourd of palm wine furnished by her family. If she was accepted and given the higher status, she would receive other household duties. This made her eligible also for the privilege of sleeping with the king. A wife usually went to him for three alternate nights. The exact rotation was decided upon by Shumba or Mankana, who kept careful tab of their co-wives, for they knew Achirimbi was not only the spiritual father of the tribe but the physical father as well. It was part of their responsibility that he keep it virile.

When he had donned fresh garments, Achirimbi ate the food prepared by one of Shumba's assistant wives. (Later, during the

1950's, he sent three wives to Nigeria. Here, in a Catholic school for domestic arts, they learned the European way of cooking.) Breakfast nearly always consisted of pounded cocoyams, palm-oil sauce with burning red pepper and other pungent spices, accompanied, of course, by tart palm wine. He seldom ate again until late in the afternoon or early evening. Unless he was at a feast, he nearly always ate alone. If he was sick, Shumba or Mankana prepared the food.

By this time the morning was half over. The king walked out on the great basalt steps of the Achum to visit with his wives who had month-old babies. A senior wife distributed wine at his direction. Then he sauntered over to meet his other wives in their yard. Periodically one would complain that he never invited her to sleep with him, but with his impish grin, he would skillfully remind her that he had nothing to say about that; she would have to speak to his top-ranking wives. The requests were varied. Some wives asked for palm oil, which the enchindas took from the imperial storehouse and distributed at the Fon's order. Perhaps a wife wished to consult him about her sick child; arrangements would be made to visit the diviner or perhaps one of the medicine men. Because the women were never allowed to be away from the royal compound overnight, any long visits to their families needed permission from the Fon. If he acceded, and he usually did, he arranged for her to take a gift of palm wine. A few of the younger women might ask permission to send a child to one of the mission schools. If these requests were granted, the entrance fees would be paid by the wife or her family, not by the Fon. His legitimate expenses he considered heavy enough; such extraneous expenditures as mission schooling he refused to pay.

All decisions were handled firmly and fairly, and they were accepted by the women without comment. Achirimbi was genuinely admired and adored by all his wives. They never forgot he was their god as well as their husband.

It was at this time of day that some of his smaller children came running up to him, throwing their arms around his ankles. They laughed and shouted and begged for food; if he was in a good humor, he bade the enchindas give them fufu. Gobbling it greedily, they scuttled back to their clamorous activities in the women's yard. This was one of the numerous scenes that made an impression on Dr. Zintgraff, for he recounted in detail how the noisy children had begged old Aboumbi for food. He didn't realize that it was one of the many games by which the Bafut people loved to amuse themselves.

About noon the chief returned to his own courtyard to hear reports from the Council of Elders. He reclined under the fig tree, with his feet resting on the ivory tusk. Across the yard the elders faced him from their seat on a low rock platform. What with a little palm wine here and there, these palavers might take all afternoon. During the day, perhaps ten or twelve townsmen would come, bringing wine and firewood. The gifts, indicating that a man had a request, were usually accepted and taken to the storehouse. When the man came in, he was offered a bit of wine by the council and a small amount of salt by one of the Fon's wives. When he left he was sure to be carrying a calabash of palm oil.

If a man wished permanent permission to speak to the king at any time, he brought an offering to the Council of Elders, ordinarily a goat and a few calabashes of wine. Thereafter, the man could greet the Fon in the ancient way, by clapping his hands three times and requesting permission to speak. If these precautions weren't observed, a fellow might be forced to stand for days without being recognized.

Of the wine, firewood, and palm oil brought to the royal compound, part of the Fon's share was divided between his wives, and part was reserved for his own use. With the many visitors, as well as the gifts that had to be sent to other areas of the grasslands, he was constantly in need of tremendous quantities of produce. When the wine gourds were overflowing, Achirimbi often invited his wives to the spacious reception hall after the evening meal. Far into the night there would be dancing, drumming, drinking, and singing. Because an evening like this usually ended with everyone feeling no pain, the wife of the evening was always selected well in advance. With the help of Shumba or Mankana, she usually succeeded in maneuvering her royal husband to the leopard-skin couch.

Achirimbi kept the promise he had made himself long ago. As soon as life returned to normal, he announced to the Bukum that he was nominating Chunga to sit on his left hand, to be his speaker and eventually to receive the title of Muma. As Achirimbi's uncle, old Muma, held that title for life, Chunga would not receive it for some years. Had no one been designated, however, Muma's first son would have assumed the position temporarily when the old man died. For several years the venerable patriarch continued to serve his nephew faithfully. Illness finally forced him to retire, thus transferring to Chunga the title as well as the functions of the office.

Ndi, Achirimbi's younger brother, was designated the adviser on his right hand, a position that became less important as the years went on. This was partly because Ndi went to the coast not long after his appointment, and also because Achirimbi was so adroit and skillful a ruler that one adviser was sufficient. Both of these appointments received the necessary approval of Kweyifon and the Council of Elders. The Fon was shrewd enough to nominate men he was sure would win endorsement.

There was another hereditary position of trust and importance reserved to royalty, and that went to the firstborn son of the king before he had been enstooled. This position, of course, went to Shumba's son, Mako, who was now a young man. From it he gained added stature in the power structure of Bafut. He applied for membership in the club made up of chiefs' sons and was immediately accepted.

The hereditary position of the queen mother was not filled; after the death of the chief's mother, this function reverted, normally, to a sister of the Fon. In the eastern grasslands, the position had been preserved and was still an important social rank. Because Ashoh was dead and Achirimbi had no sister he particularly cared to endow with the high status, Shumba and Mankana took over those duties. Besides, many men often muttered that it was not wise to allow a woman to "rule like a man."

The only other hereditary positions of royal rank in Bafut were those of the quarterheads in one or two wards. These were always given to sons of the king, and they, too, were appointed by him with the advice of the Council of Elders. The positions usually went to princes who had distinguished themselves in the society of chiefs' sons.

Following his father's precepts, Achirimbi kept in close touch with the Bukum, the Council of Elders, and Kweyifon.

This last title meant the "father of the Kweyifon," or literally, "the father of the Thing of the Chief." The name was used interchangeably for the man and the society, because the entire inner circle of the Bukum was known as the Kweyifon society. The old man was the chief executor of the Fon's orders and, naturally, he wielded prodigious influence over royal decisions. He was appointed by the Fon with the sanction of the Kweyifon society, and it was a lifetime job. (But one Kweyifon, years before, had served for about ten years when, for some unknown reason, the Council felt it would be to everyone's advantage for him to leave his post and get married. In the dead of night he was smuggled out of the country. He returned, a few weeks later, in the guise of a redeemed slave. The Fon gave him four wives, and amid great rejoicing, he returned to his compound.) With one enchinda, Kweyifon lived alone in the special hut reserved for his use in the royal compound. Here he made his sacrifices and libations to the dead ancestors. He did his own cooking, an unusual thing for a Bafut man, but much of it was augmented by daily gifts of food.

Over the years, Tahla had added to his stature in the Kweyifon society. With the consent of the Fon, through hard work, and with the payment of such fees as three goats, two gallons of wine, and ten baskets of cocoyams, he had risen steadily in the hierarchy. When the old Kweyifon succumbed to a chill during the rainy season, Achirimbi seized the opportunity to appoint Tahla to this important position. The Fon already had paved the way by assuring the council that Tahla was the best possible choice, that he would prove wise and honest, that he would exercise a firm balance to his own somewhat autocratic decisions. The Bukum was well aware of this. With few dissenting voices, they voted to raise Tahla to the second highest position in Bafut. With the entire Council of Elders as his attendants, Tahla was ushered into the presence of the king, once his associate in youthful adventure. Achirimbi grinned at him, as if to say: Now, my friend, here is your chance to do something for me— for me and for Bafut!

From that day, as high priest of the tribe, Tahla lived in the Fon's compound. He gave up his family. He was not allowed to speak directly to a woman for fear of exile. Although he could not spend the night away from the royal compound, he could visit his friends at night if he partially concealed his face with a large hat. There was no remuneration, but there were many economic advantages, for he shared in the vast tribute brought to the Fon. His sons continued to administer the trading empire he had initiated years ago.

Tahla, now Kweyifon, attended the market each week, dressed in his hood and accompanied by four or five elders, one of whom, in a loud voice, shouted the Fon's announcements. It was also Kweyifon's duty to superintend the funerals of all important men. Their estates had to be substantial, for their families were required to pay one goat, two baskets of cocoyams, and three calabashes of wine for Kweyifon's services. Religious and ritual sacrifices fell within his province, too, as did the pilgrimages to the sacred dwelling places of the dead chiefs—the only time he was gone during the night. In the name of the king he confiscated land needed for royal use by placing a special taboo marker on the property. With his two assistants, the leading Elders of the Council, he planned the religious schedule for the year, selected enchindas, chose the Fon's successor, and would inaugurate the new king should Achirimbi die.

Daily the two men conferred with each other and by their decisions shaped the future of the tribe. When the chief was absent, Kweyifon took over the reins of government. One of his most significant functions was the annual preparation of ritual medicines; for, with the Fon, he was now the protector of the entire tribe. His enormous power was magical and spiritual as well as political.

The Bukum, of which Kweyifon was a member, was composed, in traditional Tikar fashion, of nonroyalty only. But they were the select men of the tribe, economically, physically, and socially. They formed, in fact, a Bafut nobility, and they too served for life. Although a prince could not belong, he could seek permission from the society to enter his son's name on the list and pay dues for him. When the father died, the son would then become a member. If one's character and reputation were not of the highest order, ratification was withheld. Kweyifon made the final decision.

The entrance fees to the Bukum, as well as the fees for promotions to higher rank within the organization, were another way of circulating the wealth of the tribe. Many men, like Tahla, started their long journey upward through the society by serving first as enchindas. It was incumbent upon a member who was given a wife by the king to offer one of his sons for service in the enchinda group. One of Tahla's sons was already serving the Fon, but he promised several more when he became Kweyifon. Because it was presumed that he would have no more children, this was as great a sacrifice for him as it was an honor for the boys.

Achirimbi was no stranger to the economics involved in running the royal compound, the village, and the entire tribe, for Aboumbi had indoctrinated him thoroughly during the long years of training. In theory, all the land belongs to the Fon. In return for the privilege of working it and reaping its products, the villagers delivered to the king every year a part of each harvest. This occurred at the end of the harvest, the beginning of the dry season festival, which was usually held in December. The surrounding sovereign villages, those under the protection of or allied to Achirimbi, also sent in their tribute at this time. Each area had its specialty: some sent sticks on which were impaled small, dried fish and dried crabs; others sent palm oil and palm wine; a few sent meats like cutting-grass, goat, duiker, reptiles of various kinds, and occasionally a bush cow. This tribute was brought in by the subchief and presented to the intermediary, who was usually Muma or one of the chief elders. During the feast that followed, food and small gifts were exchanged. If it was nearly time for the harvest festival, the visitor would be invited to stay through the holiday.

The Fon's wives worked their own farms, but tribesmen were recruited by Kweyifon to clear the brush and perform other heavy work. In each quarter, a small emergency plot of land was eternally allocated to the Fon's special use. This plot was under the supervision of the senior wife of the quarterhead. She was known as "the mother of the compound, the bearer of children, the giver of food."

Enchindas were assigned to the Fon's two areas of palm trees to bring in the wine and oil. During the tapping season, wine was gathered each morning from the stem of the flower. Part of it was kept in a cool place to prevent fermentation. This was the sweet wine given to children and those women who preferred a milder

flavor. For stronger wine, the liquid was placed in a corked calabash and allowed to sit in the sun for a few hours. Because of its
high sugar content, it soon fermented and acquired the alcoholic
content of a strong beer. It had the consistency of water and was
cloudy white in color and slightly sour to the taste. It was rich in
iron and held no parasites. In its unfermented state, palm wine
became popular as a health drink among many Europeans on the
grasslands.

There were also hunting grounds reserved for the Fon. Each
spring Kweyifon appointed men from various wards to bring in
meat for the year. Other hunting was carried on throughout the
year, but the organized hunt for the Fon was always held in the
spring. Certain parts of the animals were traditionally reserved
for the king; some went to Kweyifon and the elders; the rest
went to the quarterheads and the hunters. In addition to the harvest, palm oil, and meat, there were great amounts of ivory in
Achirimbi's possession, for only the Fon could "hold" ivory.
It should be remembered that it was Bafut's ivory wealth that had
first attracted the Germans back in 1888.

When the British government took over in the early 1920's,
they gave each paramount chief a subsidy. In return, he collected
taxes. The male head of each family paid an amount determined
by the Fon; this was collected by one of the Bukum. Unmarried
men paid no tax, but aside from those not old enough to marry,
they were few and far between; usually they were only the
feeble-minded or the physically unsound, men unable to find a
wife.

Much of the wealth that accrued to Achirimbi was redistrib-
uted in the form of gifts and "exchanges," as well as outright
doles to the poorer men whose harvest had gone bad. But even
this largess was often paid for in the form of labor or by the service of one of the man's children. In Bafut society no one accepted
a gift without some sort of return gift, preferably one of equal
value.

Within a few years Achirimbi's compound had grown
physically, for he had accumulated even more wives, in addition
to those inherited from his father, since assuming the throne. Important men of Bafut sought his favor by giving him one of their
daughters. He could return the girl, keep her for a future wife,

or pass her on to another man, either as a favor or to repay an obligation. Enchindas were often rewarded with one of the Fon's daughters or one of these wives-in-training. The royal wives themselves were constantly on the lookout to improve their own status by finding a particularly suitable addition to the royal family.

Shumba had been told of an especially lovely girl, Lunda, who was about nine years of age. One day, after checking Lunda's lineage, to be certain she was in no way related to the Fon, she and Mankana went to the girl's father and told him of their decision. He was overjoyed at having his daughter selected for the Fon. Immediately he summoned the child to his hut so the women could mark her forehead with powdered camwood. But Lunda was out in the fields with her mother, so Shumba placed a great red daub of camwood over the door of her hut. When the girl returned to her mother's house, she was undoubtedly thrilled, for it was a great honor to be reserved for the Fon. Occasionally, however, and more so since the advent of the Europeans and mission schools (and with the advancing years of the Fon), a girl might not be overly happy with this fate. If her father gave permission—and there was really very little he could do about it—she was forced to submit. Her only recourse was to cause so much commotion in the wives' compound that they would ask to have her returned to the father. In that case, he was obligated to return the Fon's "gifts" (or their value), which were really a substitute for the bride price paid by other men. But this was most unusual.

Lunda did not go immediately to live in the palace. She remained at her father's home until she was nearly twelve. Then, escorted by her family, all of whom carried appropriate gifts, she walked to the royal compound. Here the Fon bestowed on her father favors and presents of great value, for this girl was considered of rare quality and beauty. Lunda herself was given presents of beads and cloth. The badge of royalty, a cowrie-shell bracelet, was placed around her slender wrist.

Shumba had found her, so it was Shumba who cared for the child and saw to it that, as a wife-in-training, she was taught all the important skills and rituals she needed to know as the future wife of a Fon. Much of it was hard, at first, for Lunda was little more than a servant. But when she had passed the age of puberty and began to blossom into a lovely young woman, she was given more and more responsibility. At last, when she was nearly sixteen, she was taken one night to Achirimbi's private quarters. There was no particular ceremony, but from this moment on, Lunda knew, she was truly one of the Fon's wives.

Women's societies, as such, so common throughout much of West Africa, were not usual in Bafut. However, the women from each quarter would band together to help each other at the time of a funeral, harvest, or special emergency. Wives and sisters of the Fon formed their own women's club. They danced together for the Fon, some of them playing the drums. Although this was not usual, it pleased the Fon enormously. Lunda had been taught by her father to drum well, and it was one of the devices by which she wormed her way into the Fon's affections. The wives danced together at the funerals of other royalty. A certain amount of scarification and teeth filing, usually finished before puberty, was common until the 1940's—but, again, education and Christianity made great inroads on these customs. Before Achirimbi had become Fon, many women began wearing short cotton skirts, somewhat like a sarong. The only complaint voiced by the majority of Bafut men was the high expense involved; it could be quite an investment for a man with fifteen wives and twice that many daughters.

The Grass Ceremony

Each spring the Bafut tribe commemorated an ancient Tikar custom said to be older than the Achum itself: the annual grass-thatching ceremony. This had all the trappings of a folk festival, complete with dancing, feasting, and gifts. Just as the Fon was the symbol and receptacle of power for the entire tribe, so the Achum, as the great national shrine, was the keystone of their religious worship. It was the ancient home of their ancestors, the countless dead chiefs. They, together with the living Fon, were the centrifugal force of the entire kingdom. At or near this shrine were made the decisions that affected the well-being of the community. Although one Achum might burn down, another was always built to replace it—the symbol of their ancestors, the center of the tribe.

With the Achum and the royal compound as important symbols, then, Achirimbi encouraged the grass ceremony even after a tremendous fire had destroyed part of the compound in the 1930's.

The story goes that one of the wives was careless with her cooking fire, and the flames set fire to the thatch on her hut. A strong wind soon carried the blaze throughout her side of the women's yard, and some forty or more buildings were lost. The foundations—plastered mud over raffia poles—were not destroyed, of course. Yet they were so scarred and stained from the conflagration that Achirimbi decided to have all the huts rebuilt. Tile shingles were put on some of the roofs. Galvanized sheeting had just been introduced to Bafut by the Swiss missionaries, and this was put on some buildings. This was expensive, and effective, but it was not as cool or as picturesque as the crowns of thatch on the other houses.

About this time a Swiss architect, traveling through the grasslands, visited the Swiss Basel mission on the edge of Bafut. Achirimbi commissioned him to design a new palace. He intended to keep the building for his personal use, thus leaving the Achum always accessible for religious rites. The ceremonial paraphernalia was moved to a safer place in the new palace, a handsome mud-brick building. The roof was shingled with clay tiles, making it almost immune to fire. In spite of its one-story height, it was reminiscent of a Swiss chalet, with shaded verandas running along two sides. At its base were planted a variety of tropical shrubs: dappled croton, red and yellow hibiscus, feathery, yellow allamanda, and gamboge. Along the eaves a fringe of purple bougainvillea added more color to the brilliant whitewashed building, which stood out sharply against the green trees. Flowers planted in this fashion were unusual in the grasslands, for most of the gardens were found only in the compounds of Europeans or African teachers who had been trained in the mission schools. Achirimbi worked hard to instill in his wives the same love of flowers and birds he had learned from schoolmaster Shu. Aside from the royal compound and his guest house, however, it was often a lost cause.

In the early 1940's the same Swiss architect designed an elegant resthouse on the hill just across the road from Achirimbi's palace. Here visitors to Bafut, both African and European, would find room to rest and relax, no matter how long their stay. Similar in design to Achirimbi's personal house, this one had two stories, each with its own wide veranda encircling the entire building. High above the roof was perched a cupola supporting a tall flagpole. From this the Fon's flag waved each day he was in residence. Seven rooms on each floor assured accommodations for the visitors and their servants. All the rooms but one were completely bare, for in the grasslands travelers carried all their essentials with them. The large central room on the second floor had a few massive wooden tables and chairs, products of the local trade. When it was necessary, food and firewood were carried across the road daily by Shumba or one of her assistants. This pleasant building, too, was draped with bougainvillea. It was surrounded by a spacious park with evergreens, palm trees, and orange and banana trees, the whole fenced in with shrubbery kept trim and neat by the enchindas.

When these buildings were completed and his wives' huts rebuilt, Achirimbi decided that although one reason for the grass-thatching ceremony was gone, it would be a happy occasion for everyone if it were to be continued. And so, each spring, the Achum received a handsome new roof of sweet-smelling elephant grass.

About February the men cut the tall, strong grass and bound it into conical sheaves. These were set aside for the festive day. The hunters and boys went out into the hills to find meat, and the women and girls prepared their finest gourds to be filled with sweet palm wine. Early in the fresh, cool morning, as the sun tinted the eastern sky with brilliant washes of pearl gray, scarlet, and kingfisher blue, Bafut families came trickling into the compound with their offerings. The men carried their huge pyramids of grass, one on each end of a shoulder stick. The women bore calabashes of palm wine, the precious cargo balanced on their heads with the aid of a fiber coil. The village paths echoed with tinkling laughter as the children scooted in and out of the jolly lines of people. The older boys carried fresh game across their shoulders, and the younger ones balanced small saplings on their heads. The tiniest tots brought some gift for their Fon. Dogs were shunted out of the way and goats and chickens ran noisily about.

All morning the festive throng streamed in. A few older people brought only thin wisps of grass, a token gift to the thatching ceremony. Some of them carried single sticks of fire-wood, for this, too, was essential to a well-run compound. It was all deposited in the inner courtyard and then taken to the storage huts. The crowd filed past Achirimbi, who had arranged himself with care on his carved stool beneath the fig tree. His feet, encased in magnificent beaded slippers, rested lightly on the ivory tusk. On a low table at his side was a small gourd of sweet wine. Mankana stood at his elbow to fill his horn cup with the Bafut staff of life. Regally, he poured a moderate amount from his own cup into the cupped hands of each of his subjects. As they gulped it down, they renewed their personal pledges of loyalty to the king. Even the children, on this occasion, were allowed to sip wine directly from the Fon's cup.

All morning people kept pushing into the yard until it was jammed with a noisy mass. About noon, Achirimbi announced that food would be given everyone in the outer yard, that later in the day, after the speeches, there would be the usual dancing. Then, with Mankana in attendance, he stalked into his palace to eat and to rest. In the dance plaza, baskets of pounded cocoyams, succulent fruit, and palm wine were set out. More grass was brought in and placed in a storage hut in the plaza, against the time when it would be needed.

Late in the afternoon the king returned, accompanied by several enchindas and some of his wives. Visitors had arrived: a missionary family from England. They were given seats of honor a little to the right and just below the royal platform. No one was allowed to sit on a level higher than the king. Graciously Achirimbi thanked the people for their gifts, the material to thatch his father's house, the firewood, and the food. He told them the Achum was "a blessing to all"; by honoring it in this way, glory and distinction would come to the entire tribe.

Then, turning to the visitors, Achirimbi, in pidgin English, explained the reason for this yearly ceremony. He offered them all sweet wine. Sipping it, they were surprised at its agreeable flavor. Then the door in the compound wall opened, and a group of his wives filed out, singing and shouting the praises of their husband. Achirimbi whooped vociferously. He loved a good song and dance. With a beguiling gleam in his eye, he asked the missionary's wife if she cared to join his wives as they danced. Flustered, the woman smiled uncertainly and declined; but her husband and children laughed at the chief's sense of humor.

Achirimbi jumped up from his stool and loped out to join the dancers, while his wives yelled, "Hail to thee, O Fon! Hail to thee, O Fon!" At the end of this chant, the women put their hands to their mouths, and with such volume that the hills reverberated, let out shrill war whoops, like those of the American Indian. Each time, Achirimbi roared back, "Ya, ya, ya!" He was proud of these wives, proud of their dancing and singing, proud of their ability to bear many children, proud of their well-kept fields and homes. He came back to offer more wine to the visitors. But, like many Europeans, they found it difficult to adjust to the din of the drums and the exuberance of the shouting Africans; they begged his leave to retire to his guest house. The light-hearted chief ordered Shumba to escort the visitors across the road, as he turned back to the festivities. Far into the night the singing and drumming went on, until the Fon, tired and weary with wine, started for his private house. The people straggled down the road to their own homes, leaving a silent compound under the silver stars.

A Dance for the Fon

On the first day of each week, the Bafut market was held; no work was done on that day. The fourth day of the week corresponded to the Christian Sunday, for on that day the tribe honored the living Fon; no work was performed then. The fifth day was also a quiet one, with no work carried on, because it was a day of reverence to the dead Fons. Because Aboumbi had been dead for nearly ten years, it was not as important a day as it had been in the years just following his death. Instead, the fourth day of the week now received more attention; this was the day the tribe honored their divine king and god, their living Fon, Achirimbi II. There were no special ceremonies or offerings in the homes, nor was there any general meeting. But when the people drank palm wine on this day—or brought it to the king and thus shared it—they all worshiped the monarch. Achirimbi, in turn, by drinking some of the wine presented to him, showed his deference to his dead father. It was on the fourth day of the week that a member of the Bukum could be promoted or "raised up" into a higher rank; it was on the fourth day that Achirimbi had become Fon.

Every fourth week, on this day, Kweyifon led the Council of Elders on a pilgrimage to the alternate dwelling places of the dead chiefs, the sacred pools. There were four of these, as well as sacred rocks and trees. If a pool dried up, or the water was uncommonly roiled, it was thought the spirits had left, and a deeper, darker pool in the river was sought as the new home of the deceased gods. The most significant pilgrimage was undertaken just prior to the annual four-day festival, Lela, held each year at the end of the fall harvest, usually about the third week in

December. Achirimbi never joined the pilgrims, although he discussed the journey with Kweyifon as they arranged the religious calendar for the year.

Early in the morning, with spears jingling and the double-gong sounding its hollow note, Kweyifon and a small band of elders marched some eight miles out to the river. Here, on the bank of a quiet little pool, the men gathered around their religious altar, a circle of stones set up many years before when they had moved it from Menchem Falls. There were eight stones, four called enchindas and four called wives of the Fon. Kweyifon slit open the neck of a sacrificial goat they had brought with them (in ancient times it would have been a slave) and threw it into the water. While he repeated the incantations and supplications, the elders placed a bit of powdered camwood on each stone so that when the spirit chiefs came out of the water they could rub the sacred powder on themselves. A little food and palm wine were left as an offering. When the men returned to Bafut, they were met by Achirimbi, now inwardly refreshed and strengthened by this ritual pilgrimage. In this way the old Fons bequeathed some of their energy to their successor. Later, the entire council participated in the Fon's feast.

That evening the two senior elders, assisted by other members of the Bukum, started the preparations for Lela. They draped the outer wall of the compound with Achirimbi's blue-and-white Jukun cloths. The splendid wooden ancestral figures, one male, one female, were taken from their resting place in Achirimbi's house and erected in the center of the plaza. There they remained as silent protectors throughout the four days of Lela.

Although the term *Lela* was popularly used by the Bafut as well as many other tribes throughout the grasslands, it was not entirely accurate. It meant, literally, the little flutes used in the ceremony; actually, it was the name of only the last two days of celebration. A more correct term was *the Dance for the Fon*, because the primary purpose of the entire festival was to honor the living Fon. Although they also venerated the dead chiefs, Achirimbi was the prime object of worship. Not only did the village of Bafut gather to render homage, but the other villages too throughout his sphere of influence. It was not as large a gathering as had come for the funeral of Aboumbi, but it was by far the largest assembly of each year.

On the morning of the first day of Lela, with just a scattering of observers, Kweyifon and the Council of Elders went through their opening ritual. Two Y-shaped posts were stripped of their bark and placed in the ground across from the royal compound. Kweyifon then slaughtered the sacrificial goat, taking great care to spill some of the blood at the base of each post, where a tiny altar had been placed. With his ritual knife he cut special designs and burnt them into the posts. (The Y-posts would be left in place for the rest of the year, to be moved into the Fon's compound at the next Lela ceremony, when fresh posts would be set up to receive the sacrifice. In the old days, of course, the sacrifice would have been a slave.) After this, the first palm-wine offerings, in nicely beaded gourds, modern glass pitchers, and Toby jugs, were placed before the ancestral figures.

By four o'clock in the afternoon the plaza was packed with spectators. An eerie hooting on the ivory drone trumpet signaled the opening of the festival. Kweyifon marched out of the door, striking his double-gong. Behind him were his two assistants, each blowing an ivory trumpet. The two notes rose and fell in counterpoint to each other, echoing through the village and into the hills beyond. Then the drums began, softly, slowly building up to a crescendo of pounding rhythm for the dance. Suddenly Achirimbi came out of the door and sat on his throne. Earlier in the day the leopard skin had been carefully draped over his stool, and the ivory tusk was fixed to prop up his royal feet. He wore his elephant-tail headdress and a new velvet and satin gown of blue and gold that fell in graceful folds as he waved to the cheering crowd.

Soon Mako, at the head of the society of princes and holding a dane gun stiffly before him, rushed up before his father. He bobbed his head in obeisance to the Fon, who returned the salute with a nod. Then Mako heeled and, prancing stiff-legged across the plaza, fired his gun into the air. Behind him the society of princes capered in the same manner, shooting their guns into the air, saluting and honoring the king. In turn, all the societies from the separate quarters rushed up to the chief and saluted him, singing and shouting. As he acknowledged their obeisance, they too turned and fired their dane guns into the air. Many of the fire-arms were old, by this time, and not a few men went home with wounds from a faulty gun. All this while, special songs of praises were being sung to the Fon, each secret society trying to sing louder and longer than its rivals.

Achirimbi occasionally slipped down from his throne to join the men in their dance around the field, waved to the crowd of spectators, and kept time to the drum throbs. The big signal drum as well as a tall hand drum and several smaller ones formed the orchestra for this first day. Once during the afternoon Shumba and Mankana, at the head of a long line of royal wives, danced with delicate steps around the plaza. Shumba held a beaded fly whisk, and Mankana carried a lovely tall gourd completely covered with dazzling, beaded designs. The rest of Achirimbi's wives, all carrying fly whisks, calabashes, or other ritual objects, followed them slowly, with mincing steps. As the sun poured down on the plaza, the colorful gourds flashed and sparkled. Once around the plaza they went; then they disappeared through the door in the wall.

After this, many people started dancing in a circle, saluting the king as they passed. Little children followed their parents, the tiny ones toddling and barely moving their legs, their big eyes staring in awe at the great chief. The older boys showed off with steps a trifle more intricate than those of their parents and, often as not, tripped over their own feet. The men with guns kept reloading and firing until, finally, Achirimbi stood up and with a deferential wave of his hand retired to his palace. Not long after that, the thirsty Bukum went into Kweyifon's hut for a much-needed drink. The Fon's sons and brothers gathered at the Chung hut, where they, too, quenched their thirst. Achirimbi visited each group briefly, bantering and joking with them. He teased Mako about his little son, who had fallen into the drum while trying to dance; Mako took it good-naturedly. Out in the plaza the drumming kept up for a short time, but eventually the people drifted off to their homes for the night. Later in the evening Achirimbi danced a while with his wives, but when the moon came up the village was quiet. Only the tremendous wooden ancestral figures stood mute guard over the deserted plaza.

The second day was much like the first.

Activities on the third day began, as usual, in the late afternoon, but this was the time for all military societies to salute the Fon. Achirimbi appeared in the door, his gun in hand. Chunga announced that as soon as the chief fired, the military were to answer with their shots. This was all the eager men needed to spur them on; again and again the air was blue with gunsmoke, and the mountains rang from these salutations to the living king. Then, in a gigantic circle, the men started to dance around the plaza, circling the three small drums and the little flutes called Lela. The Fon's wives came out with their fly whisks, and slipping in between the military, formed an inner circle "to make the dance fine." All were singing war songs to honor the Fon.

Suddenly Achirimbi could stand it no longer. Leaping from his stool, he rushed to the center of the plaza and joined the military societies. The spectators yelled with delight at his enthusiasm. At last, Achirimbi shouted a joke to Chunga and disappeared into the compound. This was the signal to distribute the Fon's wine to each group of military men, while the rest of the crowd slowly meandered down the village paths to their huts.

The fourth day began like the others, but there were few spectators. The Fon did not appear. Only a few Bukum and some of the better flute players performed for about an hour. Then, taking the two smaller drums, they paraded through the royal compound. The Dance for the Fon was over.

Some of the Bukum danced in the courtyard until late, joined by the king and most of his wives. Out in the plaza, the senior council members carefully removed the blue-and-white cloths and the ancestral figures and other ritual paraphernalia and stored them in Achirimbi's palace.

The Fon was the keystone of the Bafut religious and social structure. Through his sacred character he effected a power and prosperity upon all the tribe. This Dance for the Fon was a means of restoring his spiritual force, a force that he, in turn, disseminated to his people. He called upon his ancestors to witness his reign, imploring them to assure continued fertility in the land and throughout the Bafut nation.

Advancing Years

When Achirimbi inherited his father's throne, Bafut was a strong and powerful tribe, welded from such diverse groups as the original immigrant Tikar, other refugees from war and natural disasters, and captives and conquered people in the surrounding territories. A forceful and authoritative hand was needed to rule them. Aboumbi had chosen well, for Achirimbi proved to be as masterful a sovereign as his father and in some ways even more resourceful.

Within a few years, either directly or indirectly, he nearly doubled the size of the territory his father had ruled. This was accomplished by treaties, promises of protection and statements of goodwill, and the pressures applied by gifts of goods and money. Some of these gifts and exchanges included the king's daughters, his younger wives, or wives-in-training. It gave a sub-chief tremendous prestige to be united with the Fon of Bafut through a marriage alliance. But he paid for the prestige: Achirimbi had grown crafty and thrifty, and he did not lay out undue expenditures unless he was certain of receiving value for value.

On the other hand, he enjoyed an enviable reputation for hospitality—a reputation not shared by many of the other chiefs in the grasslands. Maintaining the reputation was expensive. As the result of long exposure to palm wine, the Fon was capable of imbibing great quantities at one sitting. After his introduction to European liquor, and as he became more affluent, he began lacing his wine with large draughts of whisky or gin. He knew the white men were fond of liquor, so he always offered them gin or Scotch with generous chasers of good Dutch beer. He beamed with pleasure if his hospitality was accepted. He allowed for what he considered the foibles of missionaries, and a little sadly,

he would order his wives to bring them a sweet, and slightly car-
bonated, concoction of cola or fruit squashes. As the evening became more exhilarating, he would start drinking his liquor neat.
Every white visitor to Bafut had his own story of a "night with
the Fon," but few could match the host. In spite of these baccha-
nalian nights, he was up bright and early the next morning, attending to the affairs of the tribe.

When World War II broke out, many Bafut men were on
the coast working in the rubber, cocoa, and palm-oil plantations.
These had been started by German planters back at the turn of
the century. In the peaceful lull between the two great wars, a
few Germans had come back to the Cameroons, and in return for
certain money exchanges and promises (such as good wages, education, and medical care for the African population), they were
again running the plantations. After the onslaught of September
1939, the British secret service kept them under close observation
but allowed them to go unmolested. But in May 1940, when Paris
fell to the German army, all German nationals in the British
Cameroons were quietly and efficiently rounded up and interned.
In 1942, General Jacques Leclerc arrived in Douala to lead the
Free French forces up to Fort Lamy, on Lake Chad. It was from
there they started their famous trek across the desert into Tripoli,
North Africa. The news of this epic march not only astounded
the world, but it fired the enthusiasm of the Bafut warriors, who
had long had a reputation as fierce fighters. When British recruiting officers came to ask for volunteers, Achirimbi gave them his
resthouse for a recruiting center. They did well in Bafut. Eventually many a Bafut warrior served with British Empire troops as
far afield as Egypt and Burma.

The Fon, meanwhile, carefully guided his people down the
traditional paths of strength and wisdom. He selected several
young princes to be given the kind of training he had received in
his early years, taking them on his journeys to Ndop, Banso, and
Bamenda. Several, including Mako, were sent into protective
exile in Kom and other areas.

A Native Authority Court, patterned after the British ones in
Nigeria, was located in Bafut. Achirimbi was the presiding officer. Eventually, for reasons of economy, a more central location
became imperative. The Fon hoped the court would remain in his

home village, but he was realistic enough to know that unless taxes were raised, Bafut could not afford it. The court was moved closer to Bamenda and housed in a permanent building of its own. Its president was then selected on a rotating basis. Through these courts the various chiefs determined the type and amount of construction and maintenance of roads and public buildings. They hired sanitary officers for the markets and clerks for the growing business of the Native Authority. The Native Authority Court also tried its fellow Africans for certain misdemeanors, which, for various reasons, were not taken care of in the tribal group. These were cases that crossed tribal or ethnic lines, as well as those involving British laws lately introduced to the grasslands.

One such instance involved the women who, because of modern agrarian practices, were enjoined from constructing their farm mounds vertically on the mountainsides. They had been told to place the hillocks horizontally, the better to catch and hold the water during the rains. But custom is a hard thing to change. They had placed their mounds vertically for hundreds of years, because that made it easier for them on the steep slopes. Many women were not sufficiently impressed with the superiority of the new method and so refused to fall in line. Hence, they were fined again and again by the agricultural officer. Finally, he grew tired of explaining the reasons for the change and simply reported the recalcitrants to the Native Authority Court.

Other cases, which occurred just east of Bafut, involved the Fulani people, who raised their long-horned cattle on the lush, rich grass of the Bamenda plateau. They were constantly at odds with the neighboring women farmers. The women could see no reason for fencing their farms—they had never before needed fences. The Fulani made weak attempts at keeping their cattle on the open grazing lands, but when the animals moved into the farm fields and trampled the hillocks, trouble ensued. These cases, too, wound up in the Native Authority Court, where they became a headache, primarily because of their repetitiveness. Neither side seemed to take the time to understand the reasons behind the rules. Cattle were valuable for their food value, as well as for their manure; fences were needed to assure the protection of cultivated foods.

Under the tutelage of the British District Officers, these

courts were administered primarily by the Africans themselves. It was an excellent way for Achirimbi to exert power and influence over his neighbors, yet in spite of the temptations to judicial autocracy, he became noted for his fair and impartial judgments.

The king acquired more wives, too, while losing some through death as the result of sickness or old age. It is a fair guess that during the 1950's his wives numbered between fifty and seventy-five; he himself has never admitted to more than thirty-five or forty.*

Shumba had died some years before, a victim, it was said, of one of her evil ancestors. She had been thoroughly chilled during a storm, and after that, her fabulous resistance to disease seemed to have left her.

Mankana had reached the retirement age, and she now lived quietly in the yard for senior wives. Her breasts sagged now, from bearing many children, but her woolly hair was still dark. Her voice retained its melodious timbre; she still sang and danced with gusto. From time to time she visited her many children. She greatly missed Shumba. Once in a while Mankana and the Fon reminisced about Shumba's goodness, her kindness to everyone she knew, the superb training she had given the younger wives when Achirimbi became Fon, and of how proud she had been as his first wife. Mankana knew that she herself had not many years left, but she endeavored to work a little on her farm plot. Although her daughters and granddaughters did most of the work these days, she liked to supervise them, to watch the young sprouts of corn, yams, and beans peeping up from the red earth. She insisted that if she planted the crops, surely she would live to see them harvested.

It was Shumba who had found Lunda for Achirimbi; it was Mankana who had helped with her training. The girl had risen to the top rank of wives and performed faithfully and efficiently as the number-one wife. She had grown into a tall, graceful, lithe young woman, with strong, husky thighs indicative of her years of walking over rough mountain trails. She carried her head proudly and elegantly on a neck grown strong from the balanc-

* Because of an investigation by the United Nations Committee of Women's Rights in 1949, these men became extremely chary of disclosing their true number of wives.

ing of heavy burdens. Her broad, winsome face, smooth as satin, was the color of burnished bronze. She was a true asset to the chief, for in addition to her wit and beauty, she was an excellent farmer and a crafty organizer. Lunda's father had taught her to drum. This was an exceptional skill for a Bafut girl and one that endeared her even more to her rhythm-loving husband. Lunda was one of the first to begin wearing European fashions each day. She loved gay scarves and colorful cotton cloths, and new jewels in her ears made her sparkle for days.

Lunda's marriage to the Fon had been fruitful in other ways. She had borne him a pretty daughter and then a son. The first child had been the victim of an invasion of a horde of driver ants. These vicious insects, also known as army ants, are noted in the tropics for following an unswerving path in order to reach food. They march in long, narrow columns two or three inches wide. On the outside of the column are the scouts, large black creatures half an inch long. In the center are the workers, industriously striding ahead toward food. Their speed is incredible. All of them have tremendous jaws that enable them to cling tenaciously to anything they grasp. When they find what they are seeking, food of any kind, they fan out, covering the whole territory with their big, black bodies. Their bite is extremely painful. One of the most excruciating deaths the Africans have devised is to tie a victim to a stake to be devoured by driver ants.

Lunda had left her baby with an older child, who ran out to play while the infant slept. Before anyone knew what had happened, the driver ants had nearly covered the helpless tot. The older girl's screams brought help from the few women in the yard, the enchindas, and finally from Kweyifon. To drown the ants, they thrust the baby into a dipper of water. Then each insect was pulled off with extreme care. For days Lunda gently applied oil to the wounds, but so thoroughly bitten was the little one that she never fully recovered from the attack. During the next rainy season an attack of dysentery finished her. Her death was a great blow to Lunda.

The second child, a boy, lived to be almost four. But one night, while Lunda slept with her royal husband on the leopard-skin couch, the child, alone in his mother's hut, fell into the fire. Before he could climb out and scream for help, he had been badly burned. A few days later he died. So it was extremely important to Lunda that her remaining child, a little girl who had been conceived the night of her brother's burning, receive the best education her mother could afford. In spite of her husband's reluctance, she wangled permission from him to send her daughter to the Catholic girls' school at Mamfe. The child was bright and witty, and she mirrored her mother in many ways. She was a good student. Lunda hoped, eventually, to send her abroad to study.

In spite of the grief she had known, Lunda's wide-set dark eyes nearly always smiled. But when one of the wives irritated her, they flashed angrily and became as black as night. Once, a younger wife became intrigued with the costume jewelry she found in the large market at Bamenda; she returned wearing a cheap white bracelet of plastic beads instead of the royal cowrie-shell bracelet given her by the Fon. Lunda flew into a rage, her white teeth flashing against the bronze sheen of her face. She reminded the girl that this badge of royalty was not available to every woman in Bafut, and tearing the beads off the girl's wrist, hurled them into the fire. But her anger evaporated shortly, and she was soon her usual, cheerful self again, sashaying around the compound, a true queen.

The royal compound at Bafut was gaining a reputation throughout the Cameroons as a tourist sight. In greater numbers Europeans from the coast and from Nigeria asked permission to spend a few nights in the Fon's resthouse. When the British resthouse in Bamenda was full, the manager often sent his overflow to Bafut, just fifteen miles away over a good dirt motor road. After the Fon granted the visitors permission to stay, Lunda took complete charge, collecting a small rent—which was not termed rent, for the Fon insisted that his visitors could stay as his guests. However, in return for delivering wood and sweeping the rooms with her short, palm-rib broom, Lunda, or her assistant, was given a small present, or "dash," of money. Lunda irritated the other wives by keeping this money, for they maintained that rightfully it belonged to the Fon. Some of them piously turned their cash over to him. But Lunda blithely said the Fon didn't charge the visitors rent, and thus the dash was hers to keep. No doubt Achirimbi didn't begrudge her the small amount of money, thinking it added to her salt money, and he was relieved of one more expenditure. (Salt was a precious commodity, and no one ever had enough of it. When women had a few extra pennies to spend, they often bought salt in the market. Thus, salt money was regarded as spending money.)

In the early 1950's, the village was in a continual uproar during the visit of a British naturalist, Gerald Durrell, who was collecting specimens of grassland animals for an English zoo. The two floors of the resthouse were turned over to his use. The upper floor became personal quarters for himself and his staff, and the ground floor harbored all shapes and sizes of birds and animals. "The Bafut Beagles," he called his hunters, and for years afterward men proudly introduced themselves to visitors as one of the Bafut Beagles. Achirimbi took all this in stride, for the workers were well paid, and Durrell put Bafut on the map of the world with a delightful and informative book in which he related his experiences.

The New Bafut

On the resthouse veranda, at the top of fifty cement steps, two white visitors had watched the Fon's departure for Mamfe, in his Land Rover, one day. Now they turned back to their leisurely breakfast of papaya, toast, and coffee. They were waiting for Chunga, who had promised to guide them on a tour of the village. He came, finally, carrying his walking stick in his right hand, for no Bafut went abroad without a staff to balance him on the mountain track and chase the snakes that might cross his path. With him was an interpreter, a young man with the equivalent of five or six years of schooling, who earned a few shillings here and there as official interpreter for the king. Often the white residents in the area were able to converse fairly well in pidgin English, but that required nearly six months to learn. An interpreter was almost a necessity.

Chunga took them first to the daily market, where the huge trees still protected the queen mother's grave. Here a new building for a general store was being completed. The former grass-and-fiber stall had proved insubstantial protection against the weather and an occasional thief. Once a week, on his bicycle, the ambitious storekeeper visited the larger market in Bamenda. When he returned, he balanced on his head an immense basket filled with such wares as soap, cigarettes, knives, matches, shoelaces, and a few canned goods. Also in the daily market were two "pubs," a barber shop, a bicycle-repair shop, and a hut that sheltered the corn mill. This last was a recent introduction by a young Englishwoman in the government education department; it was meant to lighten the work load of the village women. The Fon's wives liked it so well that they prevailed upon him to have one installed in his compound. On a slight rise overlooking the market was the Swiss mission church, its bell sounding melodiously, but incongruously, whenever it was necessary to call the church members to meeting.

Along the neat paths with their living fences, the visitors saw small plots of coffee trees bearing kernels and sweet-smelling blossoms on the same boughs. Some of the men augmented their subsistence economy with this new venture. The coffee kernels were dried and taken to the cooperative in Bamenda, where they were further processed. The cooperative hoped to receive enough coffee to assure a small income for each member throughout the year. A few men took their products to the British stores, where they received more money, but were also subject to the world price fluctuations.

Near the end of the path, which had now grown so narrow that a motor would have had difficulty getting through, Chunga led the visitors to a large clearing. There were two buildings, one a substantial mud-block house with a tin roof, the other an open framework of palm ribs with a thatched roof. This was the leper clinic for the village of Bafut, a part of the government Leprosy Control Program. Under the cool shade of the thatched roof were rows of benches where several men and women sat fanning themselves with banana leaves. Some puffed with satisfaction on their pipes, the women smoking tinier ones than the men. A few chewed contentedly on stinging kola nuts, spitting out the residue from time to time. These nuts contain a mild narcotic that reputedly gives one a "lift." It is from these kernels that the various cola beverages are made. Other women were tidying the grounds, pulling a few weeds here and there, and carrying water for some sprightly marigolds blooming rampant within little stone fences. Two or three women were sweeping the paths with short-handled brooms, bending double to reach the ground.

A cheerful young man came out of the large house, greeted Chunga and the interpreter, then spoke to the visitors in excellent English. This young technician, a Bafut native, had been sent by the Baptist mission to school in Nigeria, where he had been trained to dispense medicines to the clinic's outpatients. There were two large leper hospitals in the British Cameroons, one established by the Baptists in 1951 and located over the mountains not far from Kom; the other was established and directed by the

Presbyterian mission south of Mamfe. But smaller clinics, like this one in Bafut, spaced throughout the grasslands, helped in a minute way to combat the leprosy (also known as Hansen's disease) so prevalent in the tropics. The clinic was partially supported by the government as well as by the Baptist mission, in spite of the fact that the Baptists had no mission or school in Bafut.* Many lepers still hid in the bush when the doctor and his technician visited the outlying villages, for they hated to leave their homes to enter the hospital. When they did come, the whole family came with them. A considerable number were simply frightened by the white man's medicine or thought it could be of little or no help. A few families were afraid to admit that a leper was hiding among them. In recent years, however, as the lepers and their families have observed how the medicine helps combat and even cure this horrible disease, more of them have been willing to undergo treatment.

The young man invited the visitors to rest a moment while he read a passage from the Bible and led the patients in a short prayer and a hymn. After this, everyone trouped into the clinic, where the technician handed out the medicine. He gave them Dapsone, a sulfone derivative, which was taken orally twice a week. It is so effective that with it, Nigeria, a leader in leprosy research, has made great inroads in its fight against the disease. The young man made sure that each patient swallowed the pill; then he explained how it would help and how important it was for each person to return twice a week.

One little old lady bounced into the clinic with a fine new basket she had just woven and presented this as payment for her treament. If some could pay a few shillings, it was expected of them; others tidied the grounds each time they came; a few brought baskets that could be sold in the market. The mission bore the expense for those who could not pay. The World Health Organization provided the medicine free, but the mission paid the administrative costs of the supervising doctor and the equipment, and the government paid the technician's salary. Any money the patients offered was then used by the mission toward

* Years ago, the three mission groups in the British Cameroons, to avoid dissension, tacitly divided the little country into three areas and made a sincere effort to stay out of one another's sphere of influence.

fighting a few of the other diseases still found in many Africans: dysentery, filariasis, hookworm, tuberculosis, infections like yaws and jiggers, and intestinal disorders. These are just a few of the illnesses that most of the Bafut people must fight to live a normal span of years.

On the way back to the resthouse, Chunga and the interpreter took the visitors into the compound belonging to the technician. His young wife was an attractive girl whose father had been one of the first Christians in the village. She was in her yard, bathing her tiny year-old daughter in a large white porcelain bowl. She greeted the strangers soberly, and as she dried and oiled the baby, she invited the white couple to rest a moment inside her house.

It was a large house, set next to a well-kept kitchen garden and shaded by cool palms and banana trees. Being Christian, the technician had but one wife. They shared their living quarters with their three children and a younger brother. The room the visitors entered was deliciously cool after the tropical sun. It was a clean room, with a few wooden chairs scattered around a wooden table. On the wall was a church calendar, some photographs of relatives who lived in other parts of West Africa, and a large magazine picture of Queen Elizabeth with the Duke of Edinburgh.

The young woman excused herself for a moment and then returned with a tray that held a small gourd of sweet palm wine and some glasses. When the visitors looked askance at the wine, the girl explained that this was not alcoholic but new and sweet. They sipped it and found it refreshing and cool. The visitors promised to send copies of the photographs they had taken of her young husband. Then, with smiles and handshakes all around, they left the compound.

Chunga, with a chuckle, invited the young couple to visit his wives. He glanced covertly at the white woman, for he knew she would probably not approve of plural wives. She asked how many wives he had. He smiled, with the élan for which he was so noted.

"Fourteen wives and fifty or so children. But two of my wives are getting old, so I must try to find a younger one soon. My compound is very fine. I just built a new house for myself. It isn't far off the motor road. You come and my wives will have plenty palm wine and my pickens * plenty dancing."

His lively humor was infectious, and they laughed with him. He knew that if the white visitors came, they would bring presents for his wives and children. Eagerly they arranged to accept his invitation the next time they were in the vicinity. They hurried back to the resthouse to pack their belongings and return to the coast.

In the resthouse park, a blind man was being led in by a young boy, each holding the opposite end of a short length of bamboo. The interpreter explained that this young man had just returned from the Farm Craft school near Enugu in Nigeria. Here, for half of each day, he had learned how to farm though blind; the other half of the day was spent in learning a craft, such as woodworking, grass thatching, or basketry, with which he could supplement his tiny income. Some of the blindness in the grasslands is caused by filariasis and leprosy as well as by other diseases. Schools set up by the Royal Commonwealth Society for the Blind, whose headquarters are in London, helped to rehabilitate those physically able to work.† This young man lived with a married sister, and in return for his food, helped with the heavy work on her farm. For a cash income, he made wooden furniture for those who could afford to buy.

There were other signs of cultural change in Bafut. Mission schools were now scattered throughout the village. These were in addition to the two boarding schools at the outskirts, one run by the Basel Swiss Presbyterian Mission and the other by the Roman Catholics. The Basel Maternity Center was fairly well patronized by some of the Christian women. Several months prior to delivery, they reported to the Center to receive their medicine. Then about a week before the baby was due, they stayed each night in the maternity center, going out to their farms during the day. In the daily market, from one of the pubs, sounds of a rasping hand-

---

* Pidgin English for young children and babies.

† If possible, the blind boy, or a local sponsor, paid about $150 per session (one year). Most of this was for room and board, a little of it for spending money. The actual cost per person was about $1,400 per year, and this was paid by the society. If a sponsor could not be found, the society paid the entire cost.

wound phonograph could be heard from time to time; the songs were those from the coast, "Highlife" music, which was gaining in popularity.

Not to be outdone by these changes, the Fon had installed an electric motor in his sacred pool. No doubt he grinned to himself as he remembered Bisi's disaster when she tried to fetch water from the forbidden spring; but he realized what a boon it would be to his wives to have water piped into their yard. He also ordered pipes and a large storage tank placed at one end of the resthouse for the comfort and convenience of guests. This relieved the women and small boys of much drudgery, but as so often happens to motors in the tropics, the pump broke down so often that it was out of order almost as much as it was in working condition. Also in the royal compound was a rain gauge, inspected daily during the rainy season. The results were sent regularly to government officials in Bamenda.

A few years before independence, Achirimbi had learned that the British were looking for a place in the grasslands to build an airfield. In trying to combat the appalling lack of protein in the African diet, they had introduced more cattle to the plateau, in addition to those raised by the Fulani. The British hoped to open up markets on the coast. But the roads were difficult, and the lack of refrigeration made it imperative that the beef be moved quickly. Air transport was the answer. The Fon put in his bid for the airport, as he could foresee the economic advantages to Bafut. Unfortunately, a site near Bali, his ancient enemy, was chosen. The chief was forced to explore other economic avenues.

In spite of his progressive views, Achirimbi was extremely wary of harboring strangers in the village. Except for the European missionaries and a few visitors to his resthouse, no strangers were allowed to live in Bafut. He shared the Cameroons fear and distrust of the Ibo, a tribe from Eastern Nigeria, who were extremely shrewd and astute. As traders, they were to West Africa what the East Indians had become to East Africa. The Fon even refused permission for a Hausa to reside in Bafut, a man who wished to raise cattle and thus would have added to the economy.

Yet Achirimbi welcomed news from the outside. When Mount Cameroon erupted violently and destructively in 1959, the news traveled so fast through the country that the Fon knew about it within hours of the disaster. He was intrigued with this phenomenon and sent his secretary to the resthouse to ask the American visitor to come and explain how a mountain could shoot fire and ashes into the sky. Not long after that he had a chance to see the volcano himself, when he went to Buea, the tiny capital on the lower slopes of Mount Cameroon. He was one of the guests at a state dinner honoring Kwame Nkrumah, at that time prime minister of Ghana. A few months later the Fon attended the festivities held in Buea during the visit of the Duke and Duchess of Gloucester, who had been in Nigeria as representatives of the queen of England.

Independence

Eighty years is a long time in the life of any man; but to the boy who became king, eighty years has shown such a variety of events that there has been no time to worry about their passage. Life has left no visible scars but only the picture of serenity that comes from an inward composure. Time is becoming precious to him. Achirimbi, He Who Lives Eternally, can look back over eight decades and remember the shrinking of the Bafut world as foreign powers tried to seize the chief's autonomy; then, with the upheaval of world events and political changes on the entire continent of Africa, he watched his personal power again expand as the people of the grasslands sought reunion with related tribes in the former French Cameroun.

The rumblings of independence in the former colonies of European empires were heard faintly, but distinctly, on the Bamenda plateau. In the 1950's the British Cameroons, both Southern and Northern, were a United Nations trusteeship, and the day of independence seemed infinitely distant. Besides, nearly everyone took it for granted that if a final tally were taken, the people would vote to join permanently with the Nigerians, because they had been allied to them for over forty years—everyone, that is, but the people themselves.

In 1952 the Southern Cameroons had been integrated administratively with the Eastern Region of Nigeria. They held thirteen of the eighty seats in the Eastern House of Assembly at Enugu, and in the federal capitol at Lagos, they held six of thirty-four seats from the Eastern Region. They also held a post in the Nigerian Council of Ministers. Earlier, there had been criticism from the United Nations about the lack of representation from the Southern Cameroons, so these changes relieved the situation somewhat. Dr. E. M. L. Endeley, the leader of government business in the Southern Cameroons, had at the beginning supported reunification with the people of the French Cameroun. But now he urged independence for the territory as part of the Nigerian Federation. In 1954, Endeley, now premier, formed a new party, the Kamerun National Congress (K.N.C.). Having won all thirteen seats, the K.N.C. was allowed by the British government to establish the Southern Cameroons as a quasi-federal region of the Nigerian Federation. Apparently from that time on, Dr. Endeley ceased to work actively for eventual reunification with the French Cameroun. It proved his undoing.

In the spring of 1955 certain dissident spirits from the Bamenda plateau (ethnically closer to the Tikar tribes on the highlands of the French Cameroun than they were to the Bantu-related people on the coast), expressed a resentment against what they termed the "polished remoteness of Endeley and the coastal intelligentsia." These dissenters, led by John Ngu Foncha, a headmaster in a Roman Catholic School in Bamenda, were suspicious of the close ties between the K.N.C. and the Action Party in Nigeria. Dr. Endeley had already reduced, somewhat, the role of the Fons in the House of Chiefs at Buea. In addition, there was the traditional Cameroons fear and distrust of the Ibo tribe in Eastern Nigeria. This was a vague feeling not usually mentioned in news accounts of the plebiscites, but nevertheless, it was a reason expressed by many grasslands voters for wishing to reunite with the French Cameroun. Mr. Foncha and his followers formed their new party, called the Kamerun National Democratic Party (K.N.D.P.), specifically to work for the secession of the Southern Cameroons from the Nigerian Federation. At the elections in January 1959 women were for the first time given the vote.

During the days preceding this election, there was great excitement in Bafut. The Fon, one of the paramount chiefs who saw his power in the House of Chiefs being whittled away by Dr. Endeley, was preparing to throw his support to Mr. Foncha. Foncha was born and raised on the Bamenda plateau; Achirimbi felt more affinity for him and his way of thinking than for a Bakwiri man from the coast, two hundred miles away. But Endeley was an astute politician, a suave and intelligent man; he made several trips to Bafut to see the Fon and discuss with him the future of the Cameroons. The Fon received him cordially and politely listened to his arguments, apparently with an open mind. Achirimbi's tactics were always flexible, but he held unflinchingly to his principles, which to him meant only the best for his people.

Not long after Endeley's visit, the sultan of Foumban, from Bafut's traditional home in the French Cameroun, made a social call on his friend the Fon of Bafut. All the pomp and ceremony of Moslem North Africa accompanied His Highness. A long motorcade trailed into the central plaza, and then two trumpeters, holding instruments so long they had to rest them on the ground, heralded the sultan's arrival as he stepped from his auto. He was an enormous man; his elegant robe of gold-and-white brocade and white turban made him look even taller. The other men in the motorcade wore European business suits. They followed him into the great courtyard, where Achirimbi received him in a manner befitting royalty conferring with royalty. The immense crowd gathered in the plaza never knew what the two men discussed, but they were pleased and honored that so important a personage had come to visit their chief.

Election day arrived, hot and clear. Various polling places were set up throughout the village and its environs. In the royal compound, Achirimbi graciously consented to have the enchindas clean out the hut where the cornmill was normally housed, and this was used as a voting booth. Army men and neutral observers from the Cameroons Development Corporation * were sent by the government to assist with the voting. Early in the morning long lines of people began to line up outside the gate. They had been told what casting a ballot meant and how to deposit it in the box with the picture of their party choice. The incumbent party, K.N.C., used the picture of a Cameroons hut under a banana tree, and the picture of the opposition party, K.N.D.P., showed an umbrella and a palm tree.

Achirimbi came out immediately after his breakfast. He wore his large fiber hat and a nondescript Cameroons gown; cheerfully he marched up to the table, left his registration card, and entered the voting booth. When he came out of the hut, he

* A corporation formed in 1947 by Nigerian ordinance to develop the land and its resources and generally upgrade the economy of the Southern Cameroons.

playfully shook his finger at the crowd, admonishing them to vote for the proper party. The observers frowned, but the crowd yelled their appreciation of his humor.

No doubt the quarterheads had given the people orders on how the Fon wished them to vote. As far as the observers could tell, it was a secret ballot, but there was no lack of enthusiasm for the K.N.D.P. Several times during the morning a light plane flew over the village, a modern innovation that was greeted with cries of derision, for when the sheets of paper bearing the K.N.C. symbol gently floated to earth, the women and children seized them and tore them to shreds. The men laughed indulgently; they had done a good job of indoctrination.

Slowly the lines moved into the little hut. Each person held a pink registration card, which indicated the bearer was twenty-one years or more and had paid his taxes. The clerk checked his name against a typed list, then held the registration card while the voter went into the hut to cast his ballot. As he came out, the voter picked up his card and left the compound. Several old women, obviously proud of being able to take part at last in political affairs, lingered a while, clutching their cards, gesticulating with their pipes. In loud voices they said that soon they would taste the fruits of independence. The line was orderly, if vociferous. The Fon's enchindas and the Cameroons police kept the crowd in check but moving all during the day.

By four in the afternoon, everything was almost normal. The police from outlying quarters began bringing in sealed ballot boxes —two boxes, one for each party, from each voting hut. The boxes were inspected by the observers, then double-sealed, covered with brown paper, and tied with a fiber cord.

A few days later, wild rumors began to circulate. It was said that Dr. Endeley had been seen going to Wum Division with a thousand British pounds to bribe the constituents there to swing over to the side of K.N.C. Mr. Foncha and his Kamerun National Democratic Party had won thirteen of the twenty-three seats, so this rumor seemed a bit on the ridiculous side, but apparently Achirimbi thought it best to investigate. He sent by Land Rover one of his young princes to check on the rumor and see that "justice was done." It was discovered, of course, that Dr. Endeley had not visited Wum since before the election.

The new premier, Mr. Foncha, hoped for immediate secession from the Nigerian Federation. He advocated a few years of separate independence for the Southern Cameroons, probably under the aegis of the United Nations, and then reunification with the Republic of Cameroun. But the debates in the world body indicated that neither Great Britain (who would undoubtedly have had to foot the bills) nor the anticolonialist states in Africa, like Ghana and Guinea, were willing to have this possibility offered to the voters in the Southern Cameroons. In the plebiscite of May 1960 the United Nations offered only two choices: immediate reunification with the former French Cameroun (which had received its independence from France in January 1960) or a permanent integration in the Nigerian Federation.

On the first of October, 1961, the Southern Cameroons formally became the Western Region of the Federal Republic of Cameroon. Mr. Foncha, still the prime minister of the Western Region, became the vice-president of the Federal Republic. Prime Minister Amadou Ahidjo, a Moslem Peuhl from the north, moved up to the presidency. Meanwhile, the Northern Cameroons, in June 1961, had formally become a part of the Northern Region of Nigeria. Thus the two trusteeship areas reverted, more or less, to their original ethnic affiliations, from which one of them had been cut off politically for so long during the association with Great Britain.

The Southern Cameroons, released from its trusteeship protection, was thrust precipitously into union with a country that desired strong federal institutions. Foncha and Ahidjo finally agreed that the Western Region would retain a degree of autonomy over some of its internal affairs. Buea remained the capital of the Western Region. The House of Chiefs, on the verge of falling apart in Endeley's administration, was reorganized and strengthened. The Fon of Bafut served again as its president in a system of rotation. There is every indication that the K.N.D.P. has united with the larger Union Camerounaise from the Eastern Province to form one party, a party that works steadfastly and efficiently for national reconstruction.

Achirimbi, as a paramount chief in the grasslands, undoubtedly had much to say when Foncha visited him for a discussion of the path to be followed by the new country. His knowledge and advice were too valuable not to be relied upon. Both French and English are the official languages of the new republic, but because of a teacher shortage, French is still being taught only in the secondary schools of the Western Region. Bafut has requested adult-education teachers of French, and when they are available, the people will start learning another new language. Pidgin English has long been the lingua franca on the grasslands. For a while, Mr. Foncha, who gave many of his campaign speeches in pidgin, advocated that it become the official second language. Even with French and English as the two official languages in the Federal Republic, pidgin English is doing yeoman duty in some newspaper columns, a few news broadcasts (transistor radios are popular in the grasslands), and in the market place. It is also helpful in the beginning years of primary school. Educated Africans, however, are reluctant to admit its utility.

French currency is used in both regions. French laws and English laws are retained in those areas where they were first administered by the League of Nations mandate and the United Nations trusteeship. The Cameroons Development Corporation was reorganized and nationalized, and now after an initial loan from Great Britain, it is being administered entirely by Cameroonians. The Fon served for several years on its board of directors.

When the American Peace Corps was initiated in 1961, the Republic of Cameroon asked for volunteers. Peace Corps volunteers have lived for long periods in the resthouse in Bafut, most of them workers in community development. They have worked in the villages in outlying areas, helping the people construct roads, schools, and other buildings that were urgently needed. Twelve volunteers lived in Bafut in 1963. The 1964 class of Cameroon Peace Corps volunteers, all of whom went to the Western Region, numbered close to sixty. Most of them were teachers for the secondary schools, and some worked on land surveys throughout the grasslands. Also in the Republic of Cameroon were volunteers from two European Peace Corps, the Netherlands and Switzerland.

A few British nationals are returning slowly to the Western Region, to work again in the country they grew to love. A tea plantation on the eastern edge of the grasslands is doing well, producing an excellent tea for export. The airstrip at Bali is kept busy with government administrators, traders, and Peace Corps volunteers flying in from the coast. Produce is being shipped to and from the coast. Hotels have sprung up on the grasslands where once there were only a few bush resthouses with no amenities and only one catering resthouse with meager hotel facilities. The town of Bamenda now boasts a tarred, all-weather road, and two of the new hotels are located there. They are small, perhaps, with not more than twenty or thirty rooms, but they are hotels, nevertheless, where travelers can find food and shelter.

Students from the Bafut area are studying with other Western Region young people in American and English colleges and universities. They are preparing themselves in the fields of medicine, administration, government, engineering, social science, and domestic science. Their counterparts from the Eastern Region are in universities throughout France, hurrying to catch up with a world that, for so long, passed them by. Recently a college was established by the government near Bamenda. This will augment the teacher-training institutions established many years ago by the three mission groups.

Achirimbi is still vigorous, dignified, full of gentle humor and altogether irascible. He is passionately eager for the Bafut people to take their place in the new order. He can look back with satisfaction over a life whose sole purpose has now come to fruition: he has led his people into a new and different world. As they adjust to its challenges, they would be wise to listen always to the voices of their ancestors. Tradition in any culture has many practical values. There is much of it that scorns to wear the robes of evil and corruption. The tribal dignity of Bafut must not be sloughed off or held up to scorn and ridicule by the young intelligentsia. The generations to follow must learn to sift and winnow as Achirimbi and his father before him examined with discernment the new ideas introduced by the Germans and the British so long ago. The Fon's wise counsel, it is hoped, will always be remembered, for what is remembered is never lost.

Glossary

ABOUMBI (Ah-bow-OOM-be)——"He Who Rules The World," the father of the present Fon of Bafut.

ACHIRIMBI (Ah-cheer-IM-be)——"He Who Lives Eternally," the name given to the present Fon of Bafut after he assumed his throne. Before that he was called Ingwa.

ACHUM (ah-CHOOM)——The national shrine, the former dwelling place of the Fon's father, located next to the present Fon's palace.

ANLU (AHN-loo)——A women's society in Kom.

BAFUT (Bah-FOOT)——A tribe dwelling in the grassland area of the Western Region of the Federal Republic of Cameroon. They are of Tikar origin.

BAHANTAK (BAH-un-tak)——The society of royal males, sons and brothers of the Fon.

BUKUM (Boo-KOOM)——The entire Council of Elders, or any member thereof; no member of royalty is permitted to belong.

BALI (BAH-lee)——A tribe dwelling to the south of Bafut, in the grassland area of the Western Region of the Federal Republic of Cameroon, of Chamba origin.

BUSH——A country or farm area, or any wild place.

BUSH COW——A pidgin English term for forest buffalo, a dangerous animal in West Africa.

CAMWOOD——The pounded inner bark of the barwood tree of West Africa, used by many tribes for ritual purposes, such as the decoration of the person and various ritual objects. The wood from this tree is used also in the manufacture of violins and similar stringed instruments.

CHUNG——A secret society for royal males.

Cocoyam——A regional term for taro. In the grasslands it is dry taro.

Die-cry——A pidgin English term for funeral, or funeral ceremony. Sometimes called cry-die.

Enchinda——(En-CHIN-dah) Young male retainers, messengers, and servants of the Fon.

Fon (FAHN)——A paramount chief or king.

Fufu (FOO-FOO)——A pidgin English word for a farinalike mixture made of cassava or cornflour.

Juju (JOO-JOO)——A pidgin English term applied by the people to secret societies, their personnel, and equipment. In a loose sense it applies to magical and fetish devices.

Jukun (JUHK-un)——A tribe in northern Nigeria noted for its excellent blue-and-white woven cloth.

Kweyifon (KWAY-e-fahn)——Literally the "Thing of the Chief," the title given to the chief elder and right-hand man of the Fon. He is the head of the Bukum and the prime minister of the tribe.

Tikar (TEE-KAR)——The largest ethnic group in the Bamenda highlands.

Bibliography

In addition to the sources that have helped in the research of this book, the list that follows includes several other works that might be of interest to the general reader. Those marked with an asterisk (*) are now available in paperback editions. Except for the unpublished government reports, all the material can be found in any large library.

ALBERT, FATHER ANDRÉ. *Bandjoon*. Montreal: Editions de l'Arbe, 1943.

BARTH, HEINRICH. *Travels in Central Africa*, Vol. II. New York: Harper & Row, 1857.

*BOWEN, ELENOR SMITH. *Return to Laughter*. New York: Harper & Row, 1954.

BURTON, RICHARD F. *Abeokuta and the Camaroons Mountains*, Vol. II. London: 1863.

CHILVER, E. M., and P. M. KABERRY. "Traditional Government in Bafut, West Cameroon," *The Nigerian Field*, 28:1 (1963).

DAVIDSON, BASIL. *Black Mother*, The Years of the African Slave Trade. Boston: Atlantic-Little, Brown, 1961.

DELAVIGNETTE, ROBERT. *Freedom and Authority in French West Africa*. London, Oxford University Press, 1950.

*DURRELL, GERALD. *The Bafut Beagles*. London: Rupert Hart-Davis, 1954.

*GARDINIER, DAVID E. *Cameroun, United Nations Challenge to French Policy*. London, Oxford University Press, 1963.

GEBAUER, PAUL. *Spider Divination in the Cameroons*. Milwaukee: Milwaukee Public Museum, 1964.

GOVERNMENT OF SOUTHERN CAMEROONS. *Introducing the Southern Cameroons.* Lagos: Nigerian Federal Information Service, 1958.

HAWKESWORTH, E. G. *British Government Assessment Report* (unpublished). London: 1926.

HOOK, R. G. *An Intelligence Report of the Associated Village Groups Occupying the Bafut Native Authority Area, Bamenda Division, Cameroons Province* (unpublished). London: 1928 and 1934.

JEFFERIES, M. D. W. "The Bali of Bamenda," *African Studies,* *16:2* (1957).

KABERRY, PHYLLIS. *Women of the Grassfields.* London: International African Institute, 1952.

KIMBLE, GEORGE H. T. *Tropical Africa,* Vols. I and II. New York: Twentieth Century Fund, 1960.

McCULLOGH, MERRAN. *Peoples of the Central Cameroons.* London: International African Institute, 1954.

RITZENTHALER, ROBERT and PAT. *Cameroons Village.* Milwaukee: Milwaukee Public Museum, 1962.

RUDIN, HARRY F. *Germans in the Cameroons, 1884–1914.* New Haven, Conn.: Yale University Press, 1938.

*TURNBULL, COLIN M. *The Lonely African.* New York: Simon and Schuster, Inc., 1962.

ZINTGRAFF, EUGEN. *Nord Kamerun.* Berlin: 1895. (I used a précis freely translated and annotated by E. M. Chilver.)

Index